# Steps for Building an Empire of Wealth

### Lucky Vincent

ISBN-10:1500188638
ISBN-13: 978-1500188634

# DEDICATION

For Ruth my mother

the root of motherhood

And Lucky my father

the luck that follows me ever


For he who sowed the seed

but hurried ahead to sleep

And she who watered the plant

and waits for a harvest of laughters

# INTRODUCTION

Within the bindings of this book are the timeless and infallible principles that have aided all the great and wealthy men in ages past and present to build their vast empires of wealth. The principles are not based on any new philosophy, but merely a resurgence of the 'distilled wisdom of the ages'. They are the principles which have been proved and tested over the ages. We have decided to re-visit them because of the marked ignorance and lethargy that men are displaying in our societies in relation to these invaluable principles.

Glenn Bland emphatically observes: "The principles for achieving happiness and success in your life today are the same principles that King Solomon used to create his vast fortune in 966BC." He believes that only the methods have changed, but the principles remain the same. It is on this basis that we have decided to re-visit these timeless principles that have aided all great and wealthy men in ages past and present to build their vast empires of wealth.

These principles are guaranteed to aid you to successfully build your own empire of wealth. The principles worked for others. They will, no doubt, work for you too. The only thing that will be required of you is to make a firm decision and go promptly into action. If you do these, you will definitely be able to build your own empire of wealth. And the world will be glad to enjoy the fruits of your wealth.

# CONTENTS

# ACKNOWLEDGMENTS

First, I give glory to God for His inspiration and strength, and for seeing me through the writing and publishing of this book.

My sweetheart and darling wife, Emmanuella, and our lovely kids, Michael, Deborah and David, deserve my unreserved and heartfelt appreciation for the love, warmth, understanding, support, prayers and patience they have always demonstrated towards me and my writing career.

I also acknowledge all my loved ones, especially my Mum, Madam Ruth Kuti; my brothers, Mr. Christopher Obobolo, Dr. Amos Obobolo, Mr. Major Obobolo, Barr. Oviemuno (Brown) Obobolo and Mr. Samuel (a.k.a. Bonny) Ovoro; my sisters, Late Mrs. Queen Egwero, Mrs. Janet Adurosakin, Mrs. Helen Atomah, Angelina, Hannah and Faith; not forgetting all other members of the Obobolo, Idume, Egboro and Akpore families of Aviara, in Isoko South Local Government Area of Delta State, Nigeria.

I also appreciate the encouragement and support of the Management and staff of the Grundtvig International Secondary School, Oba, Delta State Polytechnic, Ozoro, University of Port Harcourt, Port Harcourt and all those who contributed in one way or the other towards the success of this book project.

I pray that God will adequately reward you all for contributing liberally towards the development of the human society

.

# PART I:
# FOUNDATION PHASE

# 1

## Believe that You Can Become Very Rich

Nobody was born with a sack of gold tied around his waist. We all came into the world stark naked. It is true that few people were born with silver spoon in their mouth, but it is equally true that all the wealth we have in the world was acquired in the process of living.

What we are driving at is the fact that we all have equal opportunity for greatness. Nobody was born to be a pauper; and nobody was born to be exclusively rich. Nobody was born to be a servant; and nobody was born to be a master. Nobody was born to be a follower; and nobody was born to exclusively be a leader. Everybody upon the face of the earth has the seed of greatness within him. You can therefore decide to be rich or to be poor; to be a master or to be a servant; to be a leader or to be a follower. The choice is yours.

And whatever choice you make depends on your belief. That is to say, belief is the starting point for all riches. Some people believe that whatever they do or whatever happens, they can never be rich. And it is certain that such people will never become rich. On the other hand, some people have established upon their mind that, comes what may, they are going to become rich and wealthy. And there is no mountain so great that can withstand such people's resolve and chances of becoming rich and wealthy.

Thus the very first thing you must do in your march towards prosperity is to renew your mind. Presently, the television of your mind, what is it showing? Is it showing failure or success? Is it showing poverty or prosperity, or is it showing average? Is it showing hardship or comfort? Is it showing suffering or enjoyment? Is it showing victory or defeat? Is it showing ill health or good health? Whatever the television of your mind is showing most of the time, that, certainly, is what you will be all the time. There is no controversy about this.

Therefore the power to become very rich and wealthy is in your hand; you hold the miracle. It is in your belief. Hebrews 11:1 says, "Now faith is the substance of things hoped for, the evidence of things not seen." What this means in relation to prosperity is that if riches and wealth are some of the things you have the hope of acquiring, your belief that you will get them transforms them into the substance that they will eventually become. That is, your belief makes the riches substantial. In other words, to borrow Napoleon Hill's words, they are transformed into their physical equivalents. That is to say, they are no more things which you are merely hoping to acquire, but they become riches that will begin to materialize.

Yes, if you have the strong belief about something, nothing can stop it from materializing. You may not have seen it at that particular time, but it is evident that it will definitely come to physical realization. Yes, you already have the evidence (living proof) of those things which you have not seen. The basic thing is for the mind to conceive and believe it. When this is done, the mind will have no option than to seek for ways of achieving what it has conceived and believed. For, whatever the mind of man can conceive and believe, the mind of man can achieve.

Therefore you must begin at the beginning. What is your belief? Do you believe that you can become very rich and wealthy, or you believe that you are going to remain poor? Or do you believe that you are going to be average and barely comfortable? If up till this moment you have not re-arranged your mindset and believe that you can become very rich and wealthy, then I must take it for granted that you have made up your mind and consented to remain a pauper or a mediocre in life.

But I must let you know that that is not the intended plan of God for your life. God intends that you may prosper. And prosperity in God's standard is unlimited. Philippians 4:19 says, "**But my God** shall supply **all** your needs **according to His riches in glory by Christ Jesus.**" If we are to comment on the highlighted words, the verse can read, "**But** (you don't need to doubt) **my God** (not your country's President or Head of State) shall supply **all** (not some of) your needs **according to His riches** (not according to the amount of money in the nation's treasury) **in glory** (not in Central Bank) **by Christ Jesus** (not by the Bank Manager, Managing Director or Governor). When you consider this, you will understand that there is no limit to the amount of prosperity or wealth that God is willing to bestow upon you.

Therefore you do not need to put yourself in a strait jacket or impose a limit upon yourself. Do you think you can become very rich and wealthy? O yes, according to His riches in glory. Do you think you can become a millionaire? O yes, according to His riches in glory. Do you think you can become a multi-millionaire? O yes, according to His riches in glory. Do you think that yours can exceed the wealth and fortune of Bill Gates of America? O yes, according to His riches in glory. The wealth of the wealthiest man on earth has limit; but the wealth and the riches of God in glory have no limit. And my God shall prosper you according to His unlimited riches in glory by Christ Jesus. This is your portion. Believe that you can become very rich and wealthy, and it shall come to pass.

# 2

## Acquire the Millionaire Mentality

To be successful, you need to be success-conscious. In the same way, to become a millionaire, you need, first of all, to acquire the millionaire mentality. What then is the millionaire mentality?

No doubt, we all know something about colonial mentality or western mentality. Most probably, all of us have been victims of colonial or western mentality. We must, at one time or the other, have prided ourselves on our ability to speak like the western man, dress like the western man or even behave like the western man. In other words, many of us have, one way or the other, tended to pattern our lifestyle after those of our western colonial masters. This is what we refer to as colonial or western mentality. In the same way, acquiring the millionaire mentality implies attempting to pattern our lifestyle after that of a millionaire.

There was a time in my life when I wanted so dearly to be a lawyer. Then, everything I did was in preparation for my entrance into the legal profession. The subjects I chose at Secondary School were such that could earn me admission to read law. But apart from this, I was beginning to assume the air and the gentlemanly way of a legal luminary. In other words, even though I was, at that period, far from being a lawyer, I was beginning to acquire the mentality of a lawyer.

At another period in my life, I desired so earnestly to be a preacher, a minister of the gospel or a public speaker. The urge was so strong that I literally assumed the lifestyle of a pastor. Then, I would walk gently like a pastor, talk sparingly like a pastor, and dress decently like a pastor. As a would-be preacher or speaker, I already saw myself preaching to multitudes. Once when I was alone in a farm, and the passion to be a speaker came so strongly and overwhelmed me, without knowing it, I literally climbed on a small hill in the farm and, assuming that the plants in the farm were my listeners, I delivered such a wonderful talk that seemingly attracted a standing ovation from my audience at the end of the presentation. If while I was standing on that hill and delivering my speech to the plants with all vigour somebody walked into the farm and saw me in that manner, he or she would immediately conclude that I had gone mad. But within me, I knew that what I was doing was acquiring the preacher or speaker's mentality.

Yes, to be a millionaire, you must, first of all, acquire the millionaire's mentality. What this means is that you must begin to assume the air and lifestyle of a millionaire. By this, I am not advocating that you become proud and arrogant as you would probably think that millionaires are. On the contrary, very rich and wealthy people are among the most humble people in the world. In most cases, they are unassuming, quite approachable and very personable.

Also, by the assumption of the air and lifestyle of a millionaire, I am not encouraging that you become a spend-thrift or an extravagant person as you would probably think that millionaires are. On the contrary, rich and wealthy people are about the most frugal and prudent people on earth. They always make sure that their hard-earned money is carefully and well spent. Rather, what I mean by the millionaire mentality or the assumption of the air and lifestyle of a millionaire is the mentality of seeing yourself as already a millionaire.

Mark Fisher, a young Canadian millionaire who wrote *The Instant Millionaire,* hinted at the importance of acquiring the millionaire mentality. In a fable in his text, Fisher writes about a man who chose to be called The Instant Millionaire, not just because he claims he became a millionaire overnight, but that he could help anyone become a millionaire overnight – or at least acquire the mentality of a millionaire.

The truth about the matter is that this man did not actually get his millions overnight. But, after being exposed to and discovering the true secret of making a fortune, the man immediately assumed the status of a millionaire in his mental faculty. That is to say, he acquired the mentality of a millionaire. Yes, the man had discovered the secret of making a fortune; he was determined to apply the secret; he knew that the secret will definitely work for him; and he knew that in a matter of time he was going to become a millionaire. Therefore he saw himself as already a millionaire. But the reality is that, then he was not yet a millionaire. He was only a potential millionaire – a millionaire in the making. But, then, he had no inhibition to being called a millionaire, knowing full well that, very soon, he was going to be a millionaire. The gist of this logic is that the man in the fable had discovered the secret of becoming a millionaire; and, in that instance, he automatically became a millionaire – at least in his mind. That is the millionaire mentality.

To become a millionaire, or to become very rich and wealthy, you must, first of all, acquire the mentality of the millionaire. Apart from the fact that it helps to fortify your belief that you can make it and become a real millionaire, it also moves you to begin to set such goals and make such plans that will eventually land you on the lot of a millionaire or even a multi-millionaire. Why not try this out and see how it works?

# 3

# Get Acquainted with the Secrets
# of Success

The Instant Millionaire in Mark Fisher's fable acquired the mentality of the millionaire only after discovering the secret to making a fortune. In the same way, it will be easier for you to acquire the millionaire mentality, and ultimately become rich and wealthy, when you are constantly exposed to sound principles and secrets of success.

The importance of the secrets of wealth is greatly emphasized when the young man in Fisher's fable is made to sign out a $25,000 cheque to the instant millionaire in exchange for the secrets. Yes, the secrets of success and wealth are worth that much, and even more. This, basically, is because, "To get rich, you have to know the secrets of wealth." They are, in fact, the guides which supply the modus operandi for playing the game. Without them, you are virtually an illiterate as far as wealth acquisition is concerned. Therefore you do not need to count the cost of how much you invest in securing those secrets. In fact, you must be willing and ready to part with a fortune in order to get the secrets of wealth.

A few years ago, I was swimming in the sea of ignorance until I was fortunate enough to discover the riches in motivational and self-development books and materials. Some of the first motivational books I bought and read include Robert Schuller's *Tough Times Never Last, But Tough People Do,* Napoleon Hill's *Think and Grow Rich,* Zig Ziglar's *Over the Top,* David J. Schwartz's *The Magic of Getting What You Want,* Glenn Bland's *Success: The Glenn Bland's Method,* Robert Schuller's *Success Is Never Ending, Failure Is Never Final,* John Mason's *Let Go of Whatever Makes You Stop,* Napoleon Hills's *Master-key to Riches,* David J. Schwartz's *The Magic of Thinking Big,* Napoleon Hill's *A Year of Growing Rich,* Dale Carnegie's *How to Win Friends and Influence People,* John C. Maxwell's *Developing the Leader Within You,* and a host of others. These, together with my regular consumption of Sunny Obazo-Ojeagbase's *Success Digest,* and the infallible word of God, *The Holy Bible,* provided the foundational knowledge of success principles and secrets upon which I have built over the years. If for no other benefits, these books and materials have not only made me to become success-conscious, but they have immensely supplied me with a repertoire of success principles and secrets of wealth that have helped me to acquire the millionaire mentality. And, today, I can boldly claim, like the man in Fisher's fable, that I have become an instant millionaire.

Yet you must realize that these secrets have and continue to cost me a fortune. As a matter of fact, I do not count the cost of whatever I spend on motivational and self-development books and materials. I can spend my last kobo on such material, knowing full well that what I stand to gain from them cannot be quantified in monetary terms. And if you, as an individual, want to make it in the real sense of it, then you must not but invest on such very rich materials.

When I say invest, I mean you must invest your money, time and effort. I have observed that some people spend a lot of money to buy books that they never read. They just keep buying and piling up books in their shelves which they never find time to read. Now I must say that such is an act of wasting both financial and material resources. In the first place, though such people are helping the authors and publishers of those books to increase their royalties and profits respectively, but they are, unfortunately, helping to remove such books out of circulation; and by so doing, doing harm to those people who are eager to buy and avail themselves of the vital knowledge that are contained in those books. Therefore if you know that you will not read a book, please do not buy it. Leave it there for the person who will buy and read it; unless, of course, you want to set up a library for others to consult.

The issue that we have been trying to stress in this chapter is the need for you to get yourself acquainted with the general principles of success, and the secrets of wealth in particular. These principles and secrets are invaluable and are greatly needed for building a worthwhile life and making significant success and progress in life's endeavours.

But you must realize that these principles and secrets are not exclusively contained in motivational books and materials. In fact, the world's greatest compendium of success principles and secrets of wealth is the Bible. Glenn Bland seems to be confirming this when he writes, "every thing you and I need to know about happiness and success is contained within the binding of one book – the Holy Bible." In Bland's view, "Within the Bible you will find the answer to all of life's opportunities and problems. It contains all of the principles found in every other book ever written about success and happiness." Perhaps you are thinking that this is an over-statement of the Bible's importance, W.E. Gladstone has this to say, "I have known ninety-five of the world's great men in my time, and of these, eighty-seven were followers of the Bible." And Glenn Bland still avers, "The principles for achieving happiness and success in your life today are the same principles that King Solomon used to create his vast fortune in 966 B.C." Therefore if really you want to achieve significant amount of success and happiness, and to acquire some good quantity of riches and wealth, you cannot do without regularly reading the Bible along with other inspirational, motivational and self-development books and materials. Within them, you will find the distilled wisdom of the ages – the principles of success and the secrets of wealth.

# 4

## Develop a Passionate Crave
## for Money

To become rich and be able to build an empire of wealth, you have to start by believing that you can, and then crave riches passionately. The very idea of having and developing a passionate crave for riches scare so many people, especially those of us in the Christian faith. Most often, we tend to equate having passion for money with the love of money. Of a truth, God, in the Bible, condemns the love of money, and sees it as the root of all evils. The truth of this is incontestable, especially bearing in mind the multiplicity of atrocities which have been engendered by the love of money in the human society. What with the armed robberies, heartless assassinations, murders, ritual killings, bribery and corruption, stealing, cheating, prostitutions, etc, which are traceable to the get-rich-quick syndrome that has pervaded our societies? Yes, these social ills and vices are, no doubt, the fallouts of the love of money.

But it must be realized that the love of money is most often motivated by loving money for its own sake. This is exhibited in the tendency to selfishly accumulate and hoard riches in such a way that they will not be useful or beneficial to the society. This, in fact, is devilish in outlook. Equally devilish is the idea of acquiring riches at all costs, irrespective of whether others are harmed or destroyed in the process or not. Yes, these forms of love for money, together with the obnoxious acts of selfishness, greed and avarice displayed by some people in their pursuits of money are what the Bible out-rightly condemns. Also condemned is the act of pursuing money with complete disregard for God and fellow man.

But having a sincere, but passionate, crave for money is quite inevitable and acceptable for acquiring such wealth that will be of benefit to the growth and development of the human society. The truth remains that, destructive as the love of money may be, money itself has served a very constructive role in the development of our societies. For one thing, civilization would probably have been impossible if money was not available to play a key role. This, probably, is why the Bible confirms, "Money answereth all things."

I think the issue at stake here is that, if a person must have a passionate crave for riches, it must be with the right motive. The person must, first of all, ask himself why he wants to accumulate money or build an empire of wealth. If the motive is merely to satisfy his selfish lust, or to feed his animal greed, or to boost his devilish ego, then there is need for him to perish the thought of building wealth. On the other hand, if the person is craving for riches because he realizes that such riches will enable him to fulfill his divinely-ordained purpose, or to contribute his own quota to the development of the human society, or towards alleviating the suffering of fellow human beings, then such a passion should be allowed to germinate and bear fruits.

Napoleon Hill, in *Think and Grow Rich,* holds, "you can never have riches in great quantities unless you can work yourself into a white heat of desire for money and actually believe you will possess it." Here, the phrase, "a white heat of desire for money", aptly describes what a passionate crave for riches is all about. It is, in fact, a burning desire for money. Unless you have a burning desire for money, you very rarely can acquire and accumulate it for the purpose of building an empire of wealth. Thus, to Hill, "A burning desire to be and to do is the starting point from which the dreamer must take off." He must, of necessity, passionately crave after riches before his dream of building an empire of wealth can become a reality.

But in craving passionately after riches, one must be on one's guard to ensure that one's passion for riches does not turn to greed and avarice, as it often does. I believe that the American society, and even the world at large, of Mrs. Henrietta Howland Green's time, was shocked more by the news of her miserly acts than by the news of her death on the 4th of July 1916. On that fateful day, *The Guinness Times* stunned the world with the news report of the death of "The World's Greatest Miser". The story reads"

> Hetty Green, reputedly America's wealthiest woman and arguably the world's most miserly, died yesterday leaving an estate worth $95 million. Mrs. Green, a New York financier who, at the age of 30 inherited

$10 million following the deaths of her father and aunt, increased this tenfold by careful management and avoiding unnecessary expenditure. Despite keeping over $31.4 million in one bank alone, Mrs. Green ate cold porridge through being thrifty to heat it, and her son's leg had to be amputated because of her delays in finding a clinic offering free medical treatment. Henrietta Howland Green (nee Robinson), born 21 Nov. 1835, New Bedford, Massachusetts; died 3 July 1916, New York City," (*Guinness Book of Records,* 1994, Pg. 146).

The above story illustrates and reveals the ease with which greed and avarice can replace a sincere and passionate crave for riches. Mrs. Henrietta Green could not even take care of herself and her son simply because of the depth of greed in her. We must also be very careful to make sure that as we are developing a passionate crave for riches, we do not allow it to become greed in us. We must be mindful of the fact that money is only a means to an end; it is not an end in itself.

# PART II:
# CAREER DEVELOPMENT PHASE

# 5

# Use Your Imagination to Generate Lucrative Ideas

The veteran motivational writer, Napoleon Hill, believes that ideas are things, and that every significant and great achievement begins with an idea. Yes, the great projects, the spectacular architectural edifices, the most complex structures, the great products and services, the well-structured organisations, the large multinationals, the great political, social and economic systems, etc, that you see around today all started as ideas in the hearts of some people.

Your ability to make a significant success in life depends largely on your ability to generate and employ good and lucrative ideas. That is to say, you can become very rich and wealthy to the extent that you are able to use your imagination to develop good business ideas and put them to profitable use. The issue of acquiring and accumulating money for the purpose of building an empire of wealth is, in a nutshell, the issue of using imagination to develop lucrative and workable ideas that could be converted to cash.

Incidentally, God has blessed everyone upon the face of the earth with imagination that is capable of generating ideas. By this, I mean that everybody possesses the ability to think. In fact, the ability to think or reason is the essence of existence and it is this that distinguishes us from animals. Yes, we all have imagination; we all have the ability to think; and we all possess the capability to reason out and generate ideas. But the onus rests on individual willingness to put imagination to use. It depends on how much of his imagination a person is able to employ for the development of such lucrative ideas that will be able to propel him from the poverty level to the level of wealth. This is not impossible. People have done it in ages past, and they are still doing it in the present age.

In ages past, people like Andrew Carnegie, John Wanamaker, George S. Parker, Henry Ford, Henry L. Doherty, George Eastman, Charles M. Schwab, Dr. Frank Gunsaulus, King Gillette, Thomas Edison, Elbert Hunnard, Judge Daniel, Orville and Wilbur Wright, Asa Candler, just to mention a few, have used their imagination to generate ideas through which they accumulated great riches and built great empires of wealth.

Apart from the fact that Andrew Carnegie became the great man of the steel industry, he, through the use of his imagination, developed the philosophy for accumulating wealth and for achieving greatness, and also sought for and developed a way of passing this great secret on to whoever cares to avail himself of it. If you have read or heard of *Think and Grow Rich* by Napoleon Hill, then you would not be ignorant of Andrew Carnegie's brain child.

And today, people like Bill Gates of Microsoft are also using their imagination to develop great ideas through which they are building great empires of wealth. Bill Gates, for instance, was once a mere University drop-out. But he was able to combine his interest in computer programming with imagination and came out with the idea of the Microsoft package. And today, he has not only built an alarmingly great empire of wealth, but has indeed emerged as the richest man in the world, netting about $5 million per hour.

Today, why not be another Andrew Carnegie who will not only develop great ideas for acquiring and accumulating wealth, but find ways of sharing such secrets with others. Or, better still, why not be another Bill Gates who will not only use a combination of interest and imagination to develop great products or services, but who will also build a vast empire of wealth. Opportunity still abounds for such a person. In fact, the world is waiting and watching out for the man of fertile imagination, and the man of great ideas. The world is waiting for the man who will come out with the idea of such a product or service that will make life easier and more enjoyable. Will you dare to be such a man?

To be such a man, you must be ready to use your imagination. People have been known to sit quietly in dark rooms for hours in order to think creatively and generate lucrative ideas. People have been known to lock themselves up in laboratories trying to work up ideas for some products or services. People have been known to walk in the woods or stand alone at sea shores all in attempts to use their imagination and generate lucrative ideas. Writers have been known to sit at their desks for hours trying to use their imagination and pens to put down ideas and philosophies that will be of benefit to humanity. Just how much of your imagination have you been able to use? Think about that!

Some people are nothing better than human robots. All they do with their lives is sleep, wake up, work, play, eat and sleep again. Such people hardly spend time to think or to use their imagination. All they want from life is to get their daily bread, and nothing more. But life is much more than being lived just to get daily bread. Life will be more fulfilling and more satisfying when we creatively use our imagination for the betterment of the human society. Think about this, if all the people in the world, from creation, have been living like robots as you are doing now, do you think that the world would have been this lovely? If people have not made deliberate efforts to generate productive and rewarding ideas, this world would, no doubt, have remained an un-nurtured wilderness.

Yes, imagination has been the singular factor that is responsible for the miraculous development that is evident in the world today. And if we need more development, then we need more men who are ready to use their imagination. In fact, the world is ready to make a way for the man who is ready to make use of his imagination. Will you dare to be that man? Will you dare to be a man of great imagination? Will you dare to be a man of lucrative business ideas? If you dare, the world will no doubt beat a path to your place of abode and heap upon you such great riches that will be enough to build you a vast empire of wealth. Dare to be the man of ideas!

# 6

## Develop Ways of Earning More

So you are earning so much? You are lucky. But wait a minute! Do you think that you have reached the limit of your earning capacity? Is there no way you can earn more than you are earning presently? Can't you, in a way, improve on or increase your earning power? These questions become more pressing considering the dwindling value of our currencies.

A casual look at the environment and circumstances around you may seem to suggest more. This is more so considering the increasing down-turn of the economy. But that will be true as far as you are looking at situations with the eye of fear. Assuredly, a more closer and positive look at the situation will surprisingly reveal various ways by which you can improve your earning or income capacity.

In fact, a man who perpetually clings to a low-paying job will eternally bemoan the dearth of money. The meager peanuts he is receiving as salary is not enough to take care of his increasing responsibilities; and he therefore remains a slave or a prisoner of circumstances, especially when he refuses to open his eyes to look and see the opportunities around him.

David J. Schwartz, in his book, *The Magic of Getting What You Want,* and Robert Schuller, in his *Tough Times Never*

*Last, But Tough People Do,* believe that you can get to wherever you want to go by taking a step in that direction. You cannot get anywhere by standing still. In the same way, you cannot see the possibility of earning more when you continue to blindly hold on to or depend wholly on a low-paying job. I am not, here, advocating that you quit your present job because of the poor remuneration. Rather, what I am trying to say is that you use your present job or source of income as a stepping stone to securing a better one.

Nobody has tied or confined you to a particular spot in life. The only thing that can stop you from releasing your potentials and from becoming the best that God wants you to be is the limit you impose upon yourself. In fact, you are unlimited, if not for your self-imposed limitations; and you are unstoppable if not for the bumps or speed-breakers that you have erected on your way to greatness.

Look around, opportunities abound as to how you can increase your earning potentials. I have read about some smart guys who joined some big organisations or corporations as messengers, but retired as Presidents or Chairmen of those organisations. I have heard of people who started out in life in abject penury, but ended up as multi-millionaires with vast empires of wealth. You are not bound to remain where you are; you are free to go from there to anywhere – it's a free world!

Are you in a low-paying job? Then seek for a better one. Or, better still, seek for ways of climbing higher up the organisation's ladder. The world is a dynamic place; and you will be left behind if you keep on standing still. Move ahead with the changing world.

Another way of increasing your income capacity is by wisely investing your savings. In fact, somebody defines capital as wealth set aside for generating further wealth. This definition more appropriately defines the role that your savings should play; it should be the wealth that you set aside for the generation of further wealth. This, in fact, is the time-tested secret of wealth accumulation. But some people see savings as the money put away against the rainy day. Yes, for small-minded people, this is so. For, as soon as there is a sign of an impending downpour, such people rush to their banks to withdraw their savings – after all, they are set aside only for the rainy day. But for the strong-minded people, savings are not for rainy days, but wealth set aside for the generation of further wealth. And the rule of the game is having a strong resolution never to touch the money, whatever happens; or a strong decision never to use it for anything except to create personal financial fortress or an empire of wealth. Have you ever considered the possibility of having multiple streams of income? This is what you should aim at having. In a nutshell, multiple streams of income is having more than one source of income.

Writing about the necessity of multiple streams of income for the present state of the economy, Robert G.Allen in *No Money Down for the 90s,* maintains, "For the 90s and beyond, one single income would not be enough to keep one going in the volatile economies around the world as we approach the millennium." Allen therefore advises that one should grow "a money tree". Allen's advice, here, is timeless, as "a money tree" is necessary not only for the '90s, but for all ages.

And Sunny Obazu-Ojeagbase avers, "In creating multiple streams of income, your objective is to have another source of income, which may not necessarily require you to lift a finger before the money comes in." Citing as an example, Obazu-Ojeagbase explains, "If you buy a share in a company operating in a growth area, like the information technology, you can guarantee that your money will make more money for you as long as the business is well managed". Another name for this sort of multiple income that Obazu-Ojeagbase is advocating is 'residual income'. You are not personally involved in the business; "all you do is hand over your money to another person or group of persons to invest and make more money for you." ("What Is Multiple Streams of Income?" *Success Digest,* May 1999, Pg. 14). Residual income is, in fact, the best form of investment. This is in the sense that it does not require your time, talents or skills, and efforts. You merely invest your money and get returns for your money, even when you are engaged in pursuing your major career. Thus it leads to effective management of your resources.

And talking about the management of your resources, one thing that a good entrepreneur or success-conscious person needs to know is the fact that everything is money. Really, to the lay people, money is not everything, but to those who want to build an empire of wealth, everything is money: time is money; talents and skills generate money; good health saves money; materials and manpower cost money; and wasted effort means wasted money. Thus, a good manager or entrepreneur makes good use of his resources. He does not make room or provision for wastage. This is because he knows that every unit of time, money, materials and efforts saved means additional income for him, and vice versa.

Having said all these, the question remains, what ways can you develop to earn more? Do you need to get a better paying job? Do you need to have further training or education in order to get promotion so as to increase your income? Don't you think you should develop some multiple streams of income, for example by engaging in some forms of trading (buying and selling) or by going into transport business or by finding a way of providing some peculiar services in your neighbourhood or try hands on some backyard business like poultry, piggery, rabbitry, fish farming, snail farming, etc? Better still, why not consider developing some forms of residual income by, say, buying shares, investing in insurance, operating a fixed deposit account, or, writing and publishing some books, or producing some audio/video CDs that could be earning you some royalties? You never can tell, that latent talent or neglected skill of yours may be what will earn you the residual income that could lift you out of poverty to the realm of wealth. Just try to find or develop a way of earning more, and your dream of building an empire of wealth will become a reality.

# 7

## Employ Your Talents and Skills

Whoever you are, wherever you are, and whatever you are doing presently, God has blessed you with a special skill or talent with which you can express yourself within the human society. And, to a very large extent, your happiness in life will depend on your ability to identify and develop this personal skill or individual talent. In fact, your skill and talent is your number one asset to be exploited in the business of building your success complex or your empire of wealth. And your inability to identify this foundational asset is the only reason why your building will not be strong or last on the sand of time.

In the whole of this wide world, there is one particular thing that you can do better than every other person in the globe. You must find out what that thing is and begin to do it immediately. If you are able to do that, there is nothing on the earth that can stop you from becoming the person that God wants you to be. One of the world's greatest inspirational writers, Napoleon Hill, puts it this way: "When the ties that bind a human mind are broken and a man is introduced to himself – the real self that has no limitations – I fancy that the gates of hell shake with fear and the bells of heaven ring with joy." (*A Year of Growing Rich*). This is not a new philosophy. It is as old as the field of human learning itself. It emanated from the ancient Aristotelian admonition: "Man, know thyself!"

Thus, one very important thing that I want you to do right now is to stop reading. Sit down quietly, and remain calm for about ten minutes. Then, think about your likes and dislikes. Try to discover what you like doing most. From what do you derive your greatest satisfaction and joy? You might have been disregarding it as something of no importance. And, all along, you might have been striving and struggling to do some other things that you think are more worthwhile. But without your knowing it, that thing that you have neglected may be your gold mine or acre of diamond. And until you go back and begin to develop that special skill or latent talent of yours, you may just be wasting your life chasing butterflies instead of digging for diamonds.

I happen to be a man who has, painfully, wasted about three and half decades of his life chasing after butterflies. Inconsistency is the word that most aptly describes my perpetual state of quandary. When I was in secondary school, I was very good in Fine Art. In fact, I was the best student in the subject in my school. My creative ability was second to none. And, to my relations, friends and classmates, I was another Leonardo da Vinci in the making. But, unknown to them, I was nursing an ambition to become a lawyer. I saw the honour and respect that legal practitioners were given in the society, and I wanted to also be a recipient of such. So, when it was time to enroll for the West African School Certificate Examination, I did not include Fine Art among my subjects. Instead, I included History with the subjects in order to get qualified for admission to read Law, as well as some science-related subjects. And, as God would have it, I passed my papers well, and I was fully qualified for Law.

But, before this time, for no cogent reason, I had lost interest completely in Law. I wanted to change to the sciences. So, the following year, I enrolled for GCE Ordinary Level, registering for such subjects as Chemistry, Agricultural Science, Biology, Economics and Mathematics. And as God would have it, I failed Chemistry, managed to have P7 in Mathematics and passed creditably Agricultural Science, Biology and Economics. The following year, I managed to gain admission into the School of Agriculture, Akure, to do a National Diploma in Agricultural Science. But I did not honour the admission because my relations were unwilling for me to read Agricultural Science; and I, too, was not deeply convinced to study that course. So, I gave up on, not only Agricultural Science, but on the sciences.

That same year, I got a job as a Store Assistant with CPI-Moore (Nig.) Ltd., Sagamu. While there, I got close to the Accountant of the Company, and I picked up interest in Accounting. I made arrangement with him and I started attending special coaching classes in Accountancy, Business Management and Economics. He was preparing me for GCE Advance Level. But before I could enroll and go for the examination, I lost the job, and that was the end of that dream.

Before this time, I had sent for a Cousin of mine who was also very good in Fine Art, and we teamed up and set up an Art Studio/Gallery. But because of wrong location and shortage of funds, the Art business did not see the light of day. It died a premature death. Then both of us had a stint of News Reporting and Newspaper Production with a local newspaper in Sagamu. It was while writing for this local newspaper that I, so to say, discovered my ingenuity and skillfulness in writing. With only the Secondary School Certificate to show as my credentials, I surprisingly distinguished myself as one of the key News Reporters and even a Columnist with the local newspaper. But my stay there was short-lived because the publisher was not faithful to the employees.

After that, I got an employment as a Textile Designer with International Laces, Alausa, Ikeja, Lagos. There, even without any formal certification that I ever did Fine Art before, I once again displayed my creative expertise in producing beautiful designs. While there, I was once again dreaming of registering for a vocational course in Art and Textile Design in order to fortify my position and status as a Textile Designer. But this dream was again nipped in the bud; for, I ran into some problem with my benefactor and mentor who, incidentally, was my boss. And I had to quit for peace to reign.

After that, I got a job with the then Lever Brothers Nig. Ltd, Ikorodu, as a Supervisor Trainee. I was beginning to settle down on the job when my Church invited me to take a full time job as the Accounting Officer of the Church. Waow! This is a dream I had cherished so much. Immediately, I threw down the training books of Lever Brothers and, before I knew what was happening, I was balancing the account books of Deeper Life Bible Church, Sagamu.

By this time, I had discovered, through the leading of the Holy Spirit, exactly what I should spend the rest of my life doing. It is something I love doing more than any other thing in the world. It is the art of putting words on paper and making books for the service of humanity. All along, this deep-rooted desire has been there. I had even made several attempts to enroll with The Writing School, London. But, in fact, I have, all along, been carried away by the glamour of other people's professions; and I have, in the process, neglected this gold mine of a talent and skill that God has given me to trade with.

So, before I even started working as an Accounting Officer to the Church, I had, upon realizing the fact that I was born to be a writer, speaker, teacher and publisher, registered for JAMB's University Matriculation Examination. And, as God would have it, I gained admission to read English at the then Bendel State University, Ekpoma. I was mad with joy. It was indeed an opportunity to get into the way of fulfilling my divinely-appointed destiny. Thus with the little stipend I earned at the Church, together with the little money I managed to beg and scavenge from Church members and relations, especially my mother, I paid my school fees, did my registrations and went to school to study the art and skill of stringing words together to bless humanity.

Within those four or five years that I was pursuing my degree programme, it is needless to say that a lot of bitter water went under the bridge. But my joy is that at this moment of going to press, I have B.A. (Hons) English, M.A. English, have completed an Executive/Professional MBA degree in order to sharpen my administrative knowledge and skill and Ph.D. Linguistics (Stylistics). I have also written and published a number of academic, motivational and inspirational books. I am just beginning, but my greatest joy is that I am, at least, doing what I love and enjoy doing more than any other thing in the world. And I am convinced far beyond reasonable doubts that, with the help of God, I will greatly excel in this area. Yes, I have been introduced to myself – the real self that knows no limitations, and nothing in this universe can stop me from making my mark in these fields of writing, speaking, teaching and publishing.

I have gone through almost the entire history of my life because I want you also to discover the special skill or talent that God has given you to profit with. If you are still doing the things that are different from your special skills and talents, then you are just wasting your life, because those things will not amount to anything worthwhile; and you will never achieve real satisfaction and happiness. So, for the umpteenth time, seek out that latent talent or special skill of yours, remove the dust from it, polish it thoroughly, develop it and begin to put it to use to the blessing of yourself, your fellow men and of God. If you can do this immediately, not even the sky will be the limit of your success.

And remember, skill must be combined with will before it can pay bills. If you have all the skills in the world but lack the will to exploit or employ them for profitable ventures, you will be worse than the person who has no skill at all. Calvin Coolidge puts it this way: "Nothing is more common than unsuccessful men with talent...unrewarded genius is almost a proverb...the world is full of educated derelicts." This observation of Coolidge is undeniable, and it is really very unfortunate.

So many people in the world are wallowing in abject poverty and failure today, not because they do not have any skill or talent with which they can express themselves and succeed, but, in most cases, they do not possess the strong will needed to use their skills up to the point of breakthrough. Many, simply, could not harness all their energy and concentrate on a central goal. In most cases, they are neither consistent nor persistent. They easily give up. But the person who will most probably make it in life is the person who possesses the strong will-power to consistently and persistently employ his God-given talents or skills until he is able to make a considerable breakthrough. Employ your talents and skills toward building an empire of wealth.

# 8

# Develop More Interest in Your Career

Whatever a person is doing, interest matters a lot. In fact, one of the major reasons why some people do badly in a particular line of business while others are doing well in the same line of business is because of their lack of interest in what they are doing. Those who are succeeding are doing so not because they are the best in that line of business, but most probably as a result of the interest with which they carry out their business.

Interest gives birth to enthusiasm. You can be enthusiastic about only what you have interest in doing. When you have no interest in something, you will not do it with enthusiasm; neither will you pursue its cause with zeal. Also, interest determines the amount of work that you will put into your business. If you are not interested in your work, career, occupation or business, you hardly will work hard at it. Instead, you will display some lackadaisical or lukewarm attitude towards the business. And under that condition, you will be working barely to earn a living. You will not derive satisfaction, joy and fun from your work; but you will begin to find your work or business both boring and burdensome. Thus, interest gives birth to enthusiasm; enthusiasm generates zeal; zeal leads to hard work; and hard work, to a large extent, brings about success.

Whatever may be the career or occupation in which you find yourself, you must endeavor to show much interest in it. It is your interest in your career or occupation that determines whether you will succeed in it or not. For one reason or the other, some people feel that they are in the wrong career or occupation. It could be that such people were forced to pursue a particular course or to enter into a particular career by the influence of their parents or relations. When this happens, the obvious outcome is that such people exhibit lack of interest in their career or occupation; hence they do very poorly.

But being disinterested in your career or occupation will not do you much good in the pursuit of success. Therefore if you discover, for whatever reason, that you do not have interest in what you are doing, there are two things you can do. You can either suspend or stop doing that thing for which you have no interest, and look for something else in which you have interest; or, better still, develop interest in that thing for which you initially had no interest.

This brings us to the consideration of the two great opportunities that you and I have at our disposal. The first opportunity is that you are not compulsorily tied to any particular career or occupation. If you do not like what you do for a living, you have every opportunity to change your mind and, even, to switch careers. Some people have had to change careers even at somewhat advanced age, and it paid off well for them. Therefore if you do not like or have interest in your present career or occupation, you do not have to force yourself against your will or desire. Instead, why not consider a change of career? You never can tell, this may be the breakthrough that you have, all the while, been praying for.

The second opportunity is that interest can be developed. The fact that you do not have interest in a particular thing now does not mean that you cannot develop interest in it. In fact, that thing or career in which you do not have interest now may be your own gold mine or acre of diamond. Therefore, throwing it away or pushing it aside because of lack of interest may not be the best option. Probably, all you need to do is to give yourself a little push and develop interest in that thing. Come on, there are some other people who are having fun doing that same thing; so why can't you? Develop interest in that career or occupation of yours and you will be glad you did. Intense interest gives enthusiasm, zeal and diligence; and you need nothing short of these for your success.

And as regards the issue of building an empire of wealth, interest in your career/occupation is a key factor. This is in the sense that your ability to acquire and accumulate money for building an empire of wealth is hinged on your success in business or career. If you are a failure in your career/business, it is very unlikely that you will be able to acquire riches. On the other hand, if you are successful in your career/business, then there is no doubt that you will acquire wealth. In other words, success in business/career invariably leads to success in acquisition of wealth.

This is where interest comes in, because, as we said earlier, you can only succeed in the business, career or occupation in which you have unalloyed interest. If interest is missing, then, assuredly, you will abysmally fail in your career, business, as well as in your resolve to build an empire of wealth. The question then is, do you have interest in your business, career or occupation? What exactly are you engaged in presently? However menial your business, career, occupation or job may seem, you do not have to despise it. What you need to do is to take it serious and to develop more interest in it. If you do this, then your dreams of achieving success, acquiring riches and building an empire of wealth will definitely become a reality.

# PART III:
# ACTION PHASE

# 9

## Stop Vacillating; Go into Action!

Have you ever read Samuel Beckett's *Waiting for Godot?* That is a work that is based on the theatre of the absurd, which parodies man's eternally vacillating nature. For one reason or the other, man is, at any point in time, waiting for something to happen first before he does what he wants to do. Yes, he wants to go back to school, but he wants to save enough money first; he wants to get married, but he wants to buy a car or build his own house first; he wants to travel out, but he wants to get married first; he wants to write a book, but he wants to get all the ideas together first; he wants to go into business, but he wants the economy to improve first; and so on, and so on, and so on. He always wants to do something, but at the end, nothing is done. That is the life of man – always vacillating.

Man is always waiting for the perfect condition to fall in place before he goes into action. Incidentally, there can never be a time when conditions will be perfect in this life. One thing or the other will always be out of place to delay a person's action. And the man who really wants to make it in life does not need to wait for perfect conditions. To him, all conditions are perfect enough for action.

Procrastination, they say, is a thief of time. And it has, indeed, stolen not only time but very many lofty dreams and projects of grandeur that would have added taste and beauty to the world. Yes, many dreams have been nipped in the bud; many plans have been left un-carried out; many projects have been abandoned all because of procrastination.

It is like the proverbial great writer who is so infatuated about a book he wants to write. Every evening, he gathers his family together and treats them to some of recipes of the beautiful stories that are to form episodes in his great book. Everywhere he goes, he narrates to whoever cares to listen very interesting and vivid descriptions of the sceneries and events from his masterpiece. He hardly can say anything or engage in any conversation without drawing the listeners' attention to his literary classic. Eventually, in the process of time, the man became very popular and famous for his great literary work.

Then, it came to pass that the man died, and he was to be buried. Very many people who have heard about his masterpiece came to pay their last respect. Many of his admirers were eager and determined to buy copies of the renown work with thousands, and even millions, of dollars. When the man's casket was eventually opened before the myriads of mourners, sympathizers and admirers, they saw the remains of the great writer as he was lain, gorgeously appareled, in the casket. Under his arms was tucked a copy of the great literary piece, with its impressive title boldly embossed. And below the glittering title is a subtitle which was meant to describe the contents of the book in a nutshell. The sentence reads: "This is the greatest book that was never written". And the family of the deceased writer explained to the perplexed mourners, sympathizers and admirers that the great book, indeed, contains nothing but blank pages of paper, from cover to cover, as the great writer wrote nothing except the impressive title. With great disappointment, all the sympathizers and admirers left one after the other, with their thousands and millions of dollars safely intact in their pockets.

This is just a fictitious story. But how well it illustrates the perpetual vacillating nature of very many people! They have some wonderful dreams, ideas or visions they want to realize; they have some beautiful plans of action to carry out; they have some great projects they want to execute. But, alas! They keep vacillating and delaying their action till the appropriate time. But, like the proverbial great writer, they carry their pet dreams, plans and projects to the grave where they are useless to the world.

Do you want to build an empire of wealth? That is a wonderful dream! Have you made a plan on how to acquire and accumulate wealth? That must be a very beautiful plan!! Do you have some projects in mind through which you can hit your millions? Those are sure to be great projects!!! But wait a minute! What are you doing right now about those dreams, plans and projects?

If, up till this moment, you are still vacillating and waiting for the appropriate time or perfect conditions, then I must tell you that those dreams, plans and projects will not do you or anybody any good. This, according to Mark

Fishers's *Instant Millionaire,* is because, "People who waste time waiting for all the perfect conditions to fall into place never get anything done." There is only one way under heaven through which you can realize your dreams; and it is BY GOING INTO ACTION. And the ideal time for action is, **RIGHT NOW!**

# 10

## Form the Habit of Taking Risks

Caution is a great word in English vocabulary. It is like a double-edged sword that cuts both ways. On the other side, it is quite advantageous when used sparingly; and on the other side, it can cause great loss when unduly emphasized.

Man, by nature, is a careful being. Right from the day of creation, man has been trying to play it safe in order not to miss the good things of life. When God told man not to touch a particular fruit in the Garden of Eden, man wanted to make sure of what he was to miss from not eating that fruit. Not wanting to take chances, he tested of the forbidden fruit, and had to face the consequences of his action. And from time immemorial, man has been naturally cautious in whatever he has to do. It is, in fact, his cautious disposition that is responsible for his perpetual tendency to vacillate.

Whatever man wants to do, he wants to, first of all, make sure that the odds are not so much against him. If he wants to go into business, he wants to make sure that there are no losses to be incurred, and that there is much profit to be made. If he wants to take any action, he wants to make sure that the consequences are favourable, not unfavourable. This explains man's tendency to look, very well, before he leaps.

But, good as the advice to "look before you leap" is, an undue over-emphasis on the looking aspect may eventually mean not leaping at all. It may be understood as an encouragement to vacillate, procrastinate or to delay action. And, as observed by the instant millionaire in Mark Fisher's fable, "People who vacillate and refuse to take risks because they don't have all the elements in hand never get anywhere." This is simply because such people do nothing and they therefore achieve nothing.

Life, itself, is risk, and it tends to favour whoever is willing to take risks. A person who wants to achieve something worthwhile in life is somebody who is ready to damn the consequences of his actions and put his back on the wall. He is that kind of person who is ready to burn all bridges and cut off all exits or routes for retreat after crossing the river to face a formidable foe in battle. Such a person is ready to either emerge victorious or die at the battlefield. He mobilizes and harnesses all available strength, strategies and inner powers to fight in order to win.

Yes, a major reason why so many people do not achieve something great in life is because they do not take great risks. And if you are among such people who are afraid of taking risks, then I must advise you to stop dreaming about achieving greatness, because that will be unattainable. To be able to attain greatness, you must be able to take great risks.

Try this out. Take time to find out the secret of the greatness of all the great people in your community, or even in the world around you. Doubtlessly, you will discover that majority, if not all of them, are great risk takers. Think about it. Such great explorers like Amerigo Vespucci and Christopher Columbus, who brought about the discovery of America; the Wright Brothers, who were the first to make and fly an aircraft; the great reformers like Martin Luther; the slave trade abolitionists like Abraham Lincoln; the great political, military, spiritual leaders, activists and freedom fighters like Mahatma Gandhi, Martin Luther King Jnr., Elijah Mohammed (Malcom X), Nelson Mandela, Julius Nyerere, Agostinho Neto, Matthew Kerekuo, Jomo Kenyata, Kenneth Kaunda, Obafemi Awolowo, Dr. Nnamdi Azikiwe, Murtala Muhammed and a host of others, have all been people who were ready to take risk; and, in fact, very many of them lost their lives in the process.

Also, great entrepreneurs and business moguls who have made tremendous impact in the business world have been people who have the ability to take risks. In fact, the second name for 'entrepreneur' is 'risk taker'. This is basically because virtually all the investment decisions that entrepreneurs make are nothing but acts of risk taking. These business investors know very well that they stand the chance of either making profit or losing their hard-earned capital. And it is even worthy of note that the money that very many of these businessmen and women use as capital in their business does not belong to them. In most cases, they are using other people's money that they borrowed from banks, finance houses or from co-operative societies;

and which must be paid back at specific periods, and some percentage of interests. All these are definitely some daring acts of risk taking.

And as it has been said and confirmed by good reason, that there can be no success without venture, it becomes mandatory for anybody who wants to acquire riches and build an empire of wealth to form the habit of taking calculated risks. He must be such a person who is capable of making prompt investment decisions regardless of what the consequences of failure may be. So, do you need loan in order to realize your dream or vision, then go ahead and obtain it; and remember to make it very big. The greater the risk, the greater will be the success that you will make out of it. This is just in line with John L. Mason's belief, "Unless you enter the beehive, you cannot take the honey"; and, "He who does not dare will not get his share". We should therefore heed Mason's advice by looking for ways of flexing our risk muscle (*Let Go of Whatever Makes You Stop*, 36).

# 11

## Work a Little Harder

God created everyone with the innate potential to succeed. But, unfortunately, majority of the people in the world today are far from being successful. This is more so when we take into consideration the poverty level of the world's population that is ever on the increase. For the technologically advanced western world, the picture is a bit consolatory; but it is a rather disheartening story to hear that virtually all the populations of the people in the underdeveloped or developing third world countries are living below the poverty line. And this is contrary to the intended plan of God for mankind.

Originally, God intended and willed that every of His creatures should prosper. But if, for one reason or the other, man is unable to appropriate this divine will for himself, then God cannot be held responsible for such failure. It is observed that there are two major reasons why this divine provision has not been fully appropriated. The first is ignorance and the second is laziness. It is sad to note that many people lack the knowledge of God's will concerning prosperity. This explains why they perpetually remain at the pit of poverty without doing anything positive to get themselves out of it. From the foregoing, it should dawn on such ignorant people that God desires the prosperity of all; and therefore expects everyone to work out his own salvation from the pit of poverty and failure to the pinnacle of prosperity and success.

To be able to do that, hard work is a must. God frowns seriously against the spirit of laziness. This, probably, is why He inspired Apostle Paul to issue the command that if any among the Thessalonian Church would not work, he should not eat also (Thessalonians 3:10). This divine command is not meant for the Thessalonian Church alone, but is, in fact, meant for every of God's creatures. It strongly reveals God's dislike for slothfulness.

It is for this that God refers the sluggard to the world's smallest, but greatest, institution of learning to obtain an M.A. degree in Diligence (Master in the Art of Diligence):

> Go to the ant, thou sluggard; consider her ways, and be wise; which having no guide, overseer, or ruler; provideth her meat in summer, and gathereth her food in harvest. How long will thou sleep, O sluggard? When wilt thou arise out of thy sleep? Yet a little sleep, a little slumber, a little folding of the hands to sleep; So shall thy poverty come as one that travelleth, and thy want as an armed man (Proverbs 6:6-11).

Yes, if you want to be free from the shackles of poverty, you must, of necessity, enroll immediately into The Art's Institute of Diligence, and begin to learn the ways of the ants. Failure to do this, it is needless to emphasize the fact that you will perpetually remain in chains right at the depth of the pit of poverty.

These days when the economy in many nations has gone so bad as a result of the global recession, and the rate of unemployment is increasingly sky-rocketing, there is the tendency for many unemployed people to bask in the excuse of joblesslessness to remain idle, go into the inglorious vocation of begging for alms, or take to crime. But there is no tenable reason for any man to resort to any of these. Whatever the case may be, man's hands can always find something worthwhile to do, especially if he takes time to look around for it. This is why the Bible admonishes that whatever your hands find to do; you should do it with all your might.

Therefore, even if you are presently unemployed, that is not enough reason for you to just sit at home and sleep. You must rise upon your feet, go out and look for something to do. Life is full of opportunities. Look out for them. It is when you have the eyes that are open for opportunities that you will be able to see and recognize them. All over the human society, as well as in our local communities, there are gaps of human needs to fill. Look out for such gaps and find a way of filling them. Particularly, look out for a job no one else wants to do and volunteer to do it. You never can tell, you may soon become a 'hot cake' in your community for doing such a job, and the money will begin to roll in.

Or, are you employed or self-employed? Then for God's sake, don's relent. That is an opportunity for you to prove your mettle. If I may repeat a good advice given by one super achiever to an anxious boy here, I would say, go and buy yourself a red shirt and work your finger to the bones. When you do that, you will be noticed by the world around you, and you will be rewarded for your hard work or diligence.

And, do you want to build an empire of wealth? Start by working hard at your job, or by being diligent at your business. If you do, you will not only succeed in building your empire of wealth, but you will also sit and dine with the crème de la crème of this world. It all begins with resolving to work a little harder than before. Try it; it pays good dividends.

# 12

## Become Smarter and Smarter Still

Become smarter and smarter still! That, no doubt, would have been an outrageous advice for the people of the Stone Age. To them, there should be no hurry in life because; slow and steady wins the race. But today, it is a known fact that the race is no longer being won by the person who runs slowly and steadily.

The reason for the above observation is obvious: the world is not standing still, but is swiftly moving on. Once upon a time, the world was in the primitive Stone Age. But today, the world has gone far beyond even the Jet Age to what we would call the Button Age. Today, you can bring the whole world right in front of you in real time merely by touching a button. This is the extent to which the resolve to make the world a global village has come in the issue of globalization. With this, the slogan 'slow and steady' is no longer in vogue. It has inevitably become obsolete. The race, and the good things of life, no longer belong to the 'slow and steady' person. Rather, they now belong to the person who can move faster and work smarter. To continue to remain 'slow and steady' is to allow the world to leave you behind and ultimately to lose the good things of life.

And, apart from the fact that the world is swiftly moving on, the truth also remains that you have only one life to live, and it is very brief. This, probably, is what the song writer has in mind when he observes that "Life at best is very brief". Therefore the earlier you realized that you do not have eternity to spend here on earth, the better for you to promptly set about doing what you ought to do in order to realize your purpose in life.

This brings to mind the memory of a beautiful nursery rhyme which we were taught in those early formative years. It says:

> Tick, says the clock
>
> Tick, tick.
>
> What you have to do
>
> Do quick

The semantic implication of this simple rhyme, unmistakably, is that time waits for no one; and that whatever a person needs to do, he should do it quickly before it becomes too late. And this, I believe, is the message for the present age. That is, as the world is racing ahead, especially in technological advancement, it behooves a man of wisdom to put on his spikes and race along with the world. This is the only thing that will make him not to be left behind in the fast-changing world.

But as you are racing along, you must need open your eyes to see the caution signs that line up the road. That is to say, it must not be a blind rush. The race must be run with care. Yes, speed is good, but it must be combined with accuracy before it can work wonders. To blindly rush ahead with disregard for caution signs on the road is to either fall into a ditch or have a head-on collision with another on-coming rusher. And this is a catastrophe that should be avoided.

Become smarter and smarter still. Good advice! But take care and watch your steps. Don't be like the careless sprinter who rushes ahead at the sound of the gun with the hope of winning the race, only to discover, as he touches the finishing tape to clinch the first position that he had run on the wrong lane. Accuracy is a necessary companion for speed. Make sure you have both, especially in this age of wonders.

And you, who wants to make millions and build an empire of wealth, you cannot but become smarter and smarter still. You must learn how to make smart moves. Really, numerous opportunities abound in this world. But the incontestable truth remains that an opportunity once lost cannot be regained. To be able to make it real good in life, you must be a man with eagle's eye for spotting opportunities and taking advantage of them.

A few years ago, some young and fresh graduates went to Lagos with eyes open for opportunities. It did not take them long before they realized that Lagos was full of rubbish heaps, with nobody caring about the job of disposing them off. Immediately, their eagle-eyes spotted the 'goldmine' in the rubbish heaps. They hired a tipper lorry and went into the business of waste disposal. And before anybody could tell what was happening, these energetic youths had turned themselves into 'hot cakes' on the streets of Lagos. And I guess they made their millions long before the imitators could come on cue.

Also, some years ago, Uren Food Processing Limited spotted a gap in the water business. Before then, people were spending N50 to buy bottled water. But, considering the poor state of the Nigerian economy and the purchasing strength of the people, they decided to go into the packaging of N5 pure water. The rate of acceptance of this product was so alarming that imitators rushed in in their multitudes. Today, the market is already over-flooded with the assorted brands of 'pure' water. And I guess that before the influx of these myriads of imitators, Uren Food Processing Limited had made her millions.

Yes, it takes smartness to be able to spot and take advantage of opportunities. And, as a man who wants to make millions and build an empire of wealth, you must endeavor to become smarter and smarter still.

# 13

## Dare to Be Desperate

Bongos Ikwe could not have been more truthful when he sang in one of his elpees that "nothing good comes easy". Obviously, Ikwe must have realized through his continuous search for fortune that it takes persistent search and continuous struggle to hit the gold. This truth continues to remain infallible as far as success in life is concerned.

To succeed in life, you do not only need to search continuously until you find and enter the road of fortune, but you also need to venture before you can make a breakthrough. Yes, if you can't venture, you can't succeed. If you can't venture, your dream of achieving success in life will be nothing but a vision in futility.

The reason for this is that progress belongs only to those who make moves. If you dream of going to America, and you do not make any move about it, it is needless to say that you will not even go as far as to the airport. In the same way, if you dream of starting a business or going to school and you do nothing about it, it goes without saying that you will long remain where you are. The simple reason for this is that you can't get anywhere by standing still. You just need to begin to take steps or make moves in order to get to places.

Success in life is synonymous to victory in a battle. In a battle, victory comes to the man who dares to strike a blow or launch an attack. Most likely, we have all heard about the story of how the little lad, David, defeated the towering giant of the Philistines, Goliath. Yes, we all know that little David came against Goliath in the name of Jehovah Nissi, the Lord of battles. But one thing that also got David the victory is that he dared to launch the first attack. In the Bible account of the incident, we see that it was Goliath who first boasted against little David, and swore to give the boy's flesh to the fowls of the air and the beasts of the field. And that was where he stopped. He did not make any move toward accomplishing his boast. Rather, he wanted to relish the effect of his boast on the little lad and on the entire army of Israel. But when the daring youth countered Goliath's bluff, he did not only vow to slay and behead the giant, but he simultaneously launched his attack by slinging a stone to hit the forehead of the awe-inspiring champion of the Philistines. That first and only attack was what gave David the victory. If David had not launched the first attack, probably the story would have been different. What we are therefore emphasizing here is that victory comes to the man who dares to strike a blow or launch an attack.

In life too, the story is not very different. Success comes to the man who dares. The man who is often timid, or who often has his tail tucked between his thighs will definitely not go far, as far as achieving success is concerned. The whole essence of entrepreneuring or doing business, for instance, is taking risks. And the man who is averse to taking risks will definitely not do well in business. Similarly, life itself is business; and to do well in the business of life, you must be a risk taker. You must be a man who dares to do things that seem impossible.

Yes, every great thing that has ever been done in this world was, at some time, thought to be impossible. It was thought impossible to fly in the air; it was thought impossible to travel to space; it was thought impossible to have light in an electric bulb or tube; it was thought impossible to transmit the human voice through the air waves; it was thought impossible to….; you name it! But today, the stories are different. The unimaginable giant stride we are experiencing in technological development today is mainly as a result of the fact that some daring people volunteered to do the seemingly impossible. And we have repeatedly been made to realize that those impossibilities are really not impossible after all. Obviously, you need to become more daring in order to do and achieve great things.

And if you really want to do great things, then you cannot help but dream great dreams. In fact, the amount of success that you will achieve in life is, to a great extent, commensurate to the greatness of your dreams. If you dream little dreams, then you will do little things and achieve little success. If you dream moderate dreams, you will do moderate things and achieve moderate success. And if you dream great dreams, then you will do great things and achieve great success. Thus your level of attainment or achievement in life is dependent on the greatness of your dream. This is purely because it is what you dream about that you will set about realizing. Therefore, the question for you now is, how great are your dreams? If you discover that they are not big enough, then I counsel you to find a way of dreaming a little bigger. Assuredly, you will achieve more for it.

But as you set about dreaming great dreams, you must make sure that you do not stop at merely dreaming. After you have dreamt your dreams, you have to set about working towards realizing them. The first step you must take in that direction is to ascertain your seriousness about the dreams. If you are not serious about something, you very rarely will do anything about it; you will perpetually delay action about it. Therefore, to be able to realize your dreams, you must not only be serious, but be desperate about it. You must desire and be determined to realize your dream with every fiber of you being. You must put yourself in such a situation that you either succeed at doing what you set out to do or you are succeeded by others who are more daring. In other words, you must give yourself no room for retreat. This is the only attitude that can guarantee you success in the realization of your dreams.

As we talk about building an empire of wealth, the tendency now is that you will look at your present condition and begin to see the impossibility of the task. But the truth remains that the goal is not unattainable, neither is the dream unrealistic. It all depends on your attitude or disposition to the task. And when you call to remembrance the fact that some people have succeeded in building their empires of wealth from the ground floor of penury upwards, then you will realize the possibility of the task. . What you need to do at this very moment is to find out from yourself whether you are serious about your dream of building an empire of wealth or not. And if you discover that you are serious, and really want to build an empire of wealth, then go a step further. Ask yourself, "Am I very desperate about this?" If you are not desperate about it, then it is doubtful if you will do anything to bring it to pass. But if you are desperate about building an empire of wealth, then you will desperately do things and work towards making it a reality, Yes, you can build an empire of wealth if you dare to be desperate about it.

# PART IV:
# WISDOM PHASE

# 14

## Concentrate on the Most Important Things

Life is full of activities. From the cradle to the grave, man is forever engaged in activities. At any period in time, he is either physically doing some things, or he is thinking or dreaming about things that he wants to do. If at any particular time you find yourself doing nothing, the only explanation for that is that you are not living. This is because in life there is no idle moment. Even at the most unproductive period when you think that you are doing nothing, your mind, nevertheless, is busy programming itself for activities. To you, you are idle, but to your mind, there is much work to do. This, probably, is why we are told in Scriptures that there is no rest for man on this side of life.

Yes, if you are to be sincere with yourself, there are so many things on your mind you want to do. But I doubt if you will ever have time enough to do all. At their face value, virtually all the things on your mind are quite necessary. But a closer look at them will, no doubt, reveal that some of them are not really that very important. To put it in Apostle Paul's language, all things (or activities) are lawful, but not all things are expedient. Some of these activities can be over-looked, and yet the equation of your life will still balance.

In fact, the limited nature of man's time demands that we select our activities in order not to be cramped or overwhelmed with too many activities, or in order not to be distracted from our major purpose. This is more so if we want to master the art of living. In this light, Apostle Paul avers, "He that striveth for the mastery is temperate in all things". What this means is that he who wants to be a master in the art of living must, of necessity, control his attitude towards things. Such a person must have self-control in the things he does and what he does not do. Put in another way, the person must exercise self-restraint in the kinds of activities he engages in.

The starting point therefore is to separate the chaff from the wheat. As we said above, there are activities that tend to distract or side-tract us from realizing our major purposes or from reaching out set goals in life. The rule is, however lawful such activities may seem, it will augur well if we can keep them at bay. We will continue to delay or deny ourselves from reaching our goals or realizing our major purposes as long as we continue to engage in such activities.

For four years after my graduation, I, for example, engaged in photography. But I knew very well that photography is not in line with my major purpose or calling in life. Rather, I knew that photography would be a distracting and hindering factor to pursuing my major calling. It did not give me enough time to write, neither did it give me the chance to make certain moves that I would have made in pursuit of my major calling. Yes, photography, at the period, was serving as a good source of income for me, and was providing me the much needed financial resources for my academic pursuits and training; but it, nevertheless, was distracting and disturbing me from concentrating on my major purpose. Yes, my intention of employing photography as a stepping stone to my real calling had paid off, but it had, notwithstanding, stood as a stumbling block to my concentrating efforts in my calling. What I therefore did, then, was to withdraw from photography as soon as my academic pursuits and training process and period was over in order to concentrate fully on the task of realizing my major purpose in life. And I thank God that I took that step.

Whatever you are doing presently, the need arises for you to channel your efforts toward fulfilling your calling and realizing your major purpose in life. First of all, you must determine whether what you are doing now is in line with your major purpose or calling in life. If it is not, then you should begin to find ways to withdraw from such activities. Those activities are important only as far as they serve as stepping stones to reaching your major calling. And even if they are important in some ways, probably you should consider employing other people to help in doing them while you concentrate your efforts only on the important things.

In order to be able to concentrate efforts on the important things, Wanda Loskot suggests "an easy way to concentrate on the productive things in your life". He says, "Every evening, write down six most important things to do the next day. Just take a piece of paper and write 'Things to do tomorrow' – 1... 2... 3... 4... 5... 6..." Loskot believes that apart from the fact that this "Six Important Things To Do" strategy provides you an opportunity to do things that really count, things that can build your self-esteem and your sense of self-expectancy, it also is the fastest road to high self-esteem and better time management. Also, Loskot believes that when you adopt this strategy,

> Your life will gradually become easier. You will experience less and less stress because fewer and fewer important things remain undone. You will realize your own abilities more often. And all of a sudden, you will find that you have much more time than ever before.

To cap it all, Loskot arithmetically calculates the productivity of those who employ his strategy thus: "Six most important things to do every day means 180 most important things to do every month. Multiply that by twelve to see how much you can accomplish in one year!" Obviously, Wanda Loskot's strategy demands a trial to ascertain its great effectiveness.

Do you want to build an empire of wealth? Do not waste your efforts on inessential things. Concentrate only on the most important things, and you will be glad you did!

# 15

## Acquire More Business Sense

Success is what everyone desires. And God also desires that everyone succeeds. One of the surest ways by which men make outstanding success in life is through business. This is more so when we are looking at success from the points of view of financial and material acquisition. Since in this text our major concern is how to build an empire of wealth, we tend to equate success with acquisition, even though we are very much aware that there is more to success than that.

Obviously, the surest and quickest way for anybody who wants early financial independence is for him to toe the line of business. This is not to say that there are no other ways of becoming financially comfortable apart from business. In fact, there are organisations that offer mouth-watering remunerations and benefits to their employees. And employees in some large and reputable multinationals rank as high as seven digits in remunerations. Yet the fact remains that salary cannot in any way be compared to the benefits accruable to business owners. This probably, is the reason why authorities in business and motivational writings opine that you can rarely become rich by working for others. Though this opinion tends to underrate the issue of working for monthly or weekly pay, but the infallible truth is that it pays much better to be your own boss.

But, good and attractive as working for yourself may be, it is often a very tough thing to do. Yes, business is tough, and it equally takes being tough to be in business. The simple reason why a large majority of people prefer to remain in salary jobs is because they prefer not to be plagued with all the headache that come from doing business. Apart from the enormous risks often involved, the strength of character, strong frame of mind and stolid physical stamina that business demands are, to many people, quite unaffordable. This is why entrepreneurship continues to remain a lonely place for the privileged few who possess what it takes to be in business.

But, however tough and challenging entrepreneurship may be, it is a career that can well launch you into the realm of the emperors of wealth. Business is tough. Agreed. But it is not inaccessible. A great number of people have made it through the same route. What I feel is required here is wisdom. Yes, wisdom, I agree, is the principal thing in business. It is not a thing for every Tom, Dick and Harry, neither is it something to dabble into by every fool who runs amok in a wild goose chase.

What we are really driving at is that it takes having some business sense to survive in the business world. It is business sense that will make you to sit down and dream out or conceive some lucrative business ideas. It is through wisdom or business sense that you are able to go out, sell your business ideas and raise the needed start-up capital for your business. It is through business sense that you will design your products or services in such a way that they become attractive to prospective customers. It is with the aid of your business sense that you formulate such marketing strategies that will enable you to penetrate even already saturated markets. It is through business sense that you can favourably compete with even established competitors. It is through business sense that you can effectively organize and manage your business profitably. It is with the aid of business sense that you re-invest or plough back your retained earnings or profits. Of a truth, business sense (or wisdom) is the number one quality to be possessed by anyone who wants to venture into the business terrains. Yes, it is through business sense that you can survive and remain in the tough terrains of business.

Unfortunately, business sense, for many of us who are even already in business, is a scarce commodity. This is evident in the outrageous decisions and actions that some of us take in the course of doing business. Some of us have perpetually remained at the bottom rung of the business ladder simply because we lack the wisdom or business sense that is needed to keep afloat on the tumultuous business sea. In some cases, some have even been forced to close shops because of apparent senselessness in the way they carry out their businesses.

There is a particular segment of Nigerians who are known for their business acumen, agility and shrewdness. These are none other than our eastern brothers and sisters. Yes, the wisdom of average Igbo man (oyen Igbo) in relation to business is second to none among the Nigerian populace. The Igbo man is patient enough to put in a number of years to serve a brother-businessman in order to learn the ropes and intricacies of the business. The Igbo man knows how to gather and save his coins until they are plenty enough for starting a little business. The Igbo man is wise enough to plough back his profit little by little until his business grows into an enviable business empire. Talk about strength of character or the strong determination that is needed for surviving in business; the Igbo man has it. Talk about the large frame of mind required for dealing with people in business; yes, the Igbo man has it. Talk about the stolid physical stamina that is necessary for handling the stress in business; oh, the Igbo man has it. Talk about the agility with which to outwit competitors and draw customers; obviously, the Igbo man has it. Talk about the shrewdness and frugality that is needed to gather in bits and in pieces; wow, the Igbo man has these in abundance. Yes, the Igbo man is a man that is built for business. He is strong, tough and has some business sense or acumen. Do you want to make it real good in business and be able to build an empire of wealth? Take a cue from the Igbo man. He is a man to watch; and he is a man to learn from. Be wise; be very wise!

# 16

## Learn to Do Things
## More Intelligently

A basic truth of life is that you can't succeed at anything unless you are doing things. The simple reason for this is that success is the sum total of the things that you do every moment of your life. To do nothing is to achieve nothing. On the other hand, to be able to achieve something worthwhile, you must, of necessity, do things.

And it is important to note that the kind of things that you do matter a lot in your bid to achieve success. For one reason, it is not everything that you do that brings you success. Rather, some things will bring you success, while some others will bring you failure, or stand in your way to success. This is the reason why we need to be careful in selecting the things that we do.

There are wrong things and there are right things. And the ready advice for all is that we endeavor to do only the right things. This is the point at which the dialectical argument as to what is right or wrong arises. The obvious question is, how do we determine what is wrong or right? Well, what is right or wrong is relative, and is dependent on the individual's perception. What I regard as right may be seen as wrong by another individual, and vice versa. Thus the issue of regarding something as right or wrong is subjective.

However, in our societies there are accepted values which if neglected, will be seen as doing the wrong thing. For instance, it is wrong in some societies for women to wear trousers, while in some societies it is acceptable. Thus the rightness or wrongness of things here is dependent on societal values. To a great extent, the values that society places on things are congruent with established principles of living. And to form the habit of doing things that society regards as wrong will most probably lead you to failure, while doing things that society approves as right will most probably lead you to success.

Nevertheless, the rightness or wrongness of the things you do, more importantly, depends on the targets or goals that you have set for yourself. In this wise, society does not have much to say in the rightness or wrongness of the things that you do. For example, a man who has set the goal of building an empire of wealth, but spends every kobo that comes his way without considering the need to set aside some percentage of his income for the purpose of wealth-building is surely doing the wrong thing. Obviously, to society, he may not be doing wrong by spending his own money; or he may not even be doing wrong things with the money. But as long as what he is doing negates his goal, then it is wrong. The question that you must ask yourself here is, "what is my goal or target in life?" After you have answered this important question, then you must check whether you are doing things in pursuance of that goal.

This is where you will know whether you are doing the wrong things or the right things. If what you are doing are not related to your set goal, then you are doing the wrong things. And such things can delay or hinder you from reaching your goal. On the other hand, if what you are doing are related to your set goals, then you are doing the right things; and such things can lead you to or quicken your journey towards your goals. It is only when you do the right things that you can get the right results.

But it is one thing to do the right things, it is quite another to do the things right. This is in the sense that it is possible to do the right things in the wrong way. Thus, how you do things matters a lot. To habitually do things foolishly or haphazardly can either delay or hinder you from reaching your goal. And to be outstanding in any area of human endeavor, you must not only do whatever you do with all your might, you must also do it intelligently. This is where wisdom comes in. To do things intelligently is to make sure not to do things 'any how'; it is taking time to do things carefully, meticulously, correctly, precisely and accurately. Also, to do things intelligently is to do things at the right time, at the right place, in the right way or manner, and for the right purpose. As we have just hinted above, wisdom is the guiding spirit that enables us to do things intelligently. Do you have it? Think about it!

As we talk about the need to do the right things at the right time, we are naturally brought to the issue of allocating time to the things that we have to do. And on this point, the Preacher, in Ecclesiastes 3:1-8, reminds us that there is time for everything and every purpose under heaven. This is to say, there is nothing you want to do here on earth that you cannot find time to do. However great or enormous that thing may be, you will always fine time enough to do it. All it takes is your ability to appropriately allocate time to it. People like Shakespeare wrote volumes of books because they allocated time to writing. And many other people have done and continue to do great and spectacular things because of adequate allocation of time to whatever they have to do in order to realize their goals. How then are you allocating time to the things that you have to do in order to reach your goal?

One of the greatest and saddest tragedies of life is that we, human beings, have continued to murder time. Hence, we do not always have time enough to do the important things that we ought to do. For those who do not know, time is un-debatably the most valuable asset on earth. Whatever else you have; if you do not have time, then you do not have anything. This is because, with time comes everything; or everything comes with time. When a person dies, what simply happens is that the person has come to the end of his time on earth; he has no more time to live. And when there is no more time like that, that person can no longer do anything. For him, time has ended. And with this sudden end of time often comes the realities of wasted time. It is at the point of death that man often realizes that there are so many things that he ought to have done but which he did not do. This belated realization often makes so many people to die regretfully and painfully.

It is so that you and I will not regret at the point of death that I am writing these words to stir you into action. Time here on earth is very brief, and it will soon pass. Within this short time of our existence here on earth, there are so many things we ought to do. And unless we wisely allocate our time to everything that needs to be done, we will continue to rob Peter to pay Paul, and we will end up accomplishing very little. For some other people, they develop the habit of perpetually struggling to kill time just when things are getting out of hands. If you find yourself in this category, remember this: he who murders sleep sleeps no more. In the same way, he who kills time has no time enough to do what he ought to do. Be wise, do the right things at the right time, and you will have no need to kill time.

It is agreed that Rome was not built in a day. But it is equally true that it did not take eternity to build Rome. Rome was eventually built because the Romans took time to do the things that needed to be done. You cannot build your empire of wealth in one day. But you do not have eternity within which to build it. You have just a short time to live. And you must do everything you ought to do within this short period of your existence. What then are the things that you ought to do in order to succeed in life, or in order to build you empire of wealth? Are you doing them now? If not, why not? Be wise; wake up and work. And as you go about doing the right things (that you ought to do) make sure you do the things right in order to get the right results. Best of luck!

# 17

## Increase Your Insight

The *Oxford English Dictionary* defines insight as: (1) Power of seeing into and understanding things; (2) Imaginative penetration; (3) Practical Knowledge; (4) Enlightenment; (5) A view into something; (6) Awareness, often of one's own mental condition (psyche); (7) The apprehension of the principle of a task, puzzle; etc. Let us look closely at two or three of these definitions of insight one after the other. The first one, the power of seeing into and understanding things, reflects a high sense of perception. It connotes a great ability to perceive the essence or the deep structure of things. This high perceptive ability is no doubt required of anybody who wants to make it real good in life. Apart from the fact that he needs to have a good understanding of the people around him, he also needs to understand the events, situations and things that are happening within his social setting. To keep a blind eye over these is to live in ignorance and be left behind.

Imaginative penetration! This reflects the sense of consciously pondering over things. Here, things are not just taken for granted. But a person consciously sits down to think about the what, why and how of things. That is, the person tends to consciously penetrate into the nature of things through the use of his imagination. In the world in which we are living today, the man who makes use of his imagination is the man who is likely to dictate the tune to others. He is the man who can know what is happening now and what is likely to happen tomorrow. Also, such a person does not only supply the ideas, but he has the practical knowledge of how to work at them.

The third and seventh definitions cited above are related in the sense that the apprehension of the principle of a task or puzzle emanates from the practical knowledge of one's task or puzzle. A person can understand how a thing works when he gets a clue to the principles or the working mechanism of that thing. Such a person is said to have the practical knowledge or insight to how the thing works. In life, the practical knowledge of how some important basic tasks, problems and puzzles are tackled is very imperative. The man who is success-bound is the man who has abundant insight into ways of doing things. He is not an ignoramus who does not know his left from his right; rather, he is a man of rich practical knowledge.

What we have tried to stress so far is the fact that insight is an important instrument for your success. If for no other purpose, it is needed for knowing what, why and how you are to do the things that are necessary for your success. In other words, you need insight in order to perform tasks, or in order to do things successfully.

The question that readily comes to mind at this point is, how can I increase my insight? Knowledge is very important for developing your insight. Thus, to increase your insight, you must do such things that can help improve your knowledge. One of such things is to read wide. The wider you read, the more knowledge you acquire, and the more insight you have into the principles of doing things. Don't just limit yourself to your discipline alone. Read other extraneous materials which are closely or remotely related to your field. This will further expose you to the various ways of doing things. Importantly, a businessman who is keen about achieving success must read materials in such related fields as Insurance, Law, Politics, Economics, Marketing, Human Resource Management, Accounting and Finance, Sociology, etc. These will no doubt expose him to the various areas in which his business could be affected.

Another thing to do in order to develop or increase your insight is to engage in practical discussions with others on important issues. This leads to the need to surround yourself with knowledgeable people. Much of what we know comes from the people around us. Nobody can know anything if the people around do not know anything. It is the people around us who give us information about the happenings around us, and about how to do things for which we do not possess the know-how. The whole essence of education is having people to teach us what we do not know. Thus a basic thing to do in order to develop insight is to acquire education. To do this is to surround ourselves with such books and knowledgeable persons that can teach us things which we do not know.

And to be able to do this is to keep an open mind for new ideas and new ways of doing things. A person who has a parochial or narrow mind about ideas and things will, no doubt, have very low insight about how to do or go about things. And it takes having an open mind to learn from others. Also, it takes humility to be taught. A proud and arrogant person is very unlikely to learn from others, and he is very likely to have very low insight about things, ideas and situations. Thus the hallmarks for developing insight are open-mindedness and humility. Do you have them? Think about it.

Still on the issue of increasing your insight, there is the need for you to acquire or develop new skills. You do not know how to do things until you learn how to do them. One of the things that will give you a sense of fulfillment in life is, giving yourself the task of acquiring a new skill every now and then. In the days of old, one of the marks of greatness and of an accomplished life is the ability to do a great variety of things. It will be a great injustice to the present age if we relegate the importance of accomplishment to the past alone. Thus, today, a man who is skillful and talented in a variety of things commands some good amount of respect and admiration within his community. Besides, such a person derives satisfaction and joy from performing those peculiar and exclusive things. You, also, need to strive towards fulfillment and accomplishment by resolving to learn and acquire new and important skills regularly and periodically. When you do that, you are on the way to increasing your insight; and most importantly, you are also on the road to stardom.

Experience, they say, is the best teacher. And to develop your insight, you must rely greatly on your past experience. Unless you are a day-old baby, you must have behind you years, months, weeks or days of rich life experiences. Within your past are a variety of events, situations and things in which you have failed or succeeded; been sad or happy; sorrowful or joyful; praised or condemned, etc. Yes, your past contains a well-stocked archive rich with the principles of how to or how not to do things. These principles of life that are derivable from your past experiences serve as sources of knowledge from which you can draw at will. They thus also serve as means for increasing your insight into the nature, structure or working mechanism of things, events and situations. And the longer you have lived on earth, the greater the wealth of knowledge that you can draw from your past experiences. What we are trying to emphasize here is the need for you to resolve to learn much from experience in order to increase your insight. Experience is a great teacher.

Having been exposed to some of the ways of developing or increasing your insight, the need also arises for you to know the secret of insightful thinking. Already, you have been told that insight connotes imaginative penetration into the nature of things; and that the person in question consciously sits down to ponder over the what, why and how of the things, events and situations around him. The major reason for doing this is to gain control over those events, situations and things – to know the principles of life and master the art of living.

This, again, brings us in contact with one of the greatest principles of successful living: "In quietness lies your strength". The truth of this principle lies in the fact that it is at the sacred moment of quietness that you release your mind to consciously and meticulously ponder over the nature of things, events and situations. At this moment, the mind wants to grasp the basic mechanisms that are responsible for the happenings around – the mind wants to gain insight into life and living. And when the mind is able to do this, it does not only derive the strength (stamina and boldness) with which to confront the events, situations and things; it also acquires the wisdom needed for successful living. This is the secret of insightful thinking.

As we talk about the practical steps for building an empire of wealth, our discussion will not be complete if we do not repeatedly emphasize the necessity of stretching your imagination for that singular purpose. This is the pivot of

Napoleon Hill's principles for growing rich. To acquire riches and be able to build an empire of wealth, you must develop the habit of consciously thinking through to wealth. You must task your imagination and continuously ponder over the what, why and how of wealth-building. Like the businessman, you must seek out and read through all related materials on the subject of wealth. You must surround yourself with books and persons who are knowledgeable in the art of wealth-building. And you must be open-minded and humble enough to learn new and lucrative ways of building wealth. More importantly, you must rely on your past experiences, as you already know from it what works and what does not work. Again, you must sit down and employ your imagination for thinking through to wealth. When you do all these, you will not only gain insight into the art of wealth building, but you will actually set about laying your blocks one after the other in the act of building an empire of wealth.

# PART V:
# MONEY HANDLING PHASE

# 18

## Reduce Your Spending

You may not be earning so much money, but that is not to say that you cannot become rich and wealthy. It all depends on how you handle the little or meager financial resources that come your way. Yes, your becoming rich and wealthy does not depend so much on the fatness of your paycheck, neither does it greatly depend on the size of your profit margin. The level of your income is not the determining factor for getting rich and wealthy.

As we have just said above, what you do with what you get matters a lot in the issue of building wealth. It does not really matter whether you are getting so much or so little. What makes the difference is whether you are consuming all that you get or conserving part of it. This reminds me of the story of a young man who was my colleague at a printing firm where I first worked after my secondary school education. Ugolo was a handsome, hardworking and very wise young man. In fact, I can say he was wiser than all of us who were up-coming youngsters at the factory. His wisdom was particularly evident in his frugal disposition and in his self-discipline.

For the rest of us, it was a different story. Probably, we felt that we were still very young, and that we were earning some good money. So during every break time, all of us would file out of the company's premises and go to a nearby restaurant where each of us would, thoughtlessly, order for and devour plates of expensive food, with bottles of drink to match. We believed then that we needed to enjoy our lives to the fullest from the labour of our hands. But as for Ugolo, his break time was always better spent resting, sleeping, meditating, reading some religious materials (especially *Awake* or *The Watchtower*, since he was a member of Jehovah Witness) or just discussing some basic issues of life or religion with some of us who returned early from our lunch outing. Ugolo would never go out there and take part in the thoughtless spending; and he never criticized anyone for doing so.

Eventually, before our very eyes, Ugolo got married and also bought a car. It was unbelievable. How can a person who was a junior staff like us, and whose salary was so small get married and at the same time buy a car? It was really very unbelievable. But we all knew that Ugolo had planned, sacrificed and saved towards it and had eventually got it. After some time, Ugolo resigned from the Company and went into transportation business. Later, he was able to gather enough money to set up his own printing press. The last time I saw him, he was having three cars and his business was doing quite well. Since then, we have lost contact for about three decades now. Presently, I don't know how he is doing, but I believe that, going by the speed he was moving, he must be a very big business man now.

What about those of us who were enjoying life some twenty five to thirty five years ago in that Company? Well, I have also lost contact with virtually all. But, going by the kind of lifestyle we adopted at that time, I will not be surprised if many of us are still out there struggling to eke out a living from the harsh realities of life. And many of us are, most probably, bowing down to our bosses as employees, while Ugolo is bossing around in his own little business empire as an employer of labour. Such is life, you may say!

But what you can glean from the above story and from all that has been said so far in this text is, you don't have to part with all your money living in pleasure and luxury. Rather, you should form the habit of conserving part of your earning by finding ways of cutting cost or reducing your spending so as to succeed in your plan of building an empire of wealth.

Whatever may be the level of your spending presently, it can still be reduced. All you need to do is to check or cut off your buying of inessential things. In fact, the habit of buying things negates the habit of saving. Materialism and luxury are at variance with wealth accumulation. Thus, the starting point for building an empire of wealth is for you to cut down on your buying. The logic is, you either buy things now or keep your money for the purpose of building an empire of wealth so that you can have better things later.

And apart from the need for you to buy only things that are essential, you must of necessity discontinue the habit of buying things on impulse. In fact, this is one way in which a great majority of people waste a lot of money. As they walk along the street or as they window-shop around the market or supermarket, they buy whatever catches their fancy on impulse. This habit of making unplanned-for expenses is a sign of indiscipline. As a disciplined individual, you don't have to buy things on impulse. Rather, your buying habit should be constrained by a budget. Endeavour to periodically draw up a budget of your expenses and try as much as possible to stick strictly to it. Also, you must try to make a priority list of your needs and follow it to the letter. And, if you must buy anything on impulse, it must be within the limit of the amount of money earmarked for miscellaneous expenses in your budget.

But if you want to stop the habit of buying things on impulse, there are two things you have to do:

1. Stop the habit of window-shopping. If you do not want to buy anything, then you have no business roaming around markets and supermarkets. And, as you move along commercial streets, mind what your eyes see; and even when you see some attractive and desirable things, pretend not to see them, or don't think about what you see. Instead, concentrate on where you are going.
2. Stop the habit of carrying huge amount of money on you. When your pocket is lean, there is a limit to what your mind would tell you to buy.

One other thing you must do in order to reduce your spending is to form the habit of buying essential commodities in bulk. Bulk purchase, at the point of buying, may seem as if the person is spending a lot of money. But on the long run, it pays off better than having to buy in small quantities every now and then. Obviously, bulk buying is cheaper than buying piece meal and it saves money.

It is a little difficult task having to point out all the areas where you have to reduce your spending. I guess it will be much more effective if personal self-examination is done on the issue. We all know the areas where we have been victims of undisciplined over-spending. All we need to do is to identify such areas and be determined to have a check on them. But the basic thing is that we constantly keep in mind our goal of building an empire of wealth. If this really is our goal or target, then we should always be reminded that we cannot make it a reality if we continue to indulge in the habit of over-spending. Let us not be penny wise and pound foolish!

# 19

## Develop a Systematic Saving Scheme

In the "Step by Step Guide to Financial Freedom" published in the September 1997 issue of *Success Digest,* Brian Tracy, one of the *Insight* authors, supplies 10 reasons and steps that have made millions of men and women who started with nothing but ended up rich and retired financially independent. Tracy believes that "By learning and practicing these 10 simple principles, you can retire financially independent as well. They are:

1. Make a decision that you are going to become financially independent.
2. Set a goal for yourself.
3. Make detailed plans.
4. Develop a systematic saving scheme.
5. Carefully, wisely invest the money you are saving.
6. Study, research and investigate financial opportunities.
7. Get out of debt and stay out of debt.
8. Continually look for ways of increasing or adding value to what you do.
9. Resolve never to touch the money you are putting away whatever happens.
10. Never give up.

No doubt, we have already said one or two things about virtually all the above principles for financial independence that Brian Tracy advocates. But it is necessary that we take a closer look at some of them, especially the one that talks about developing a systematic saving scheme. By now, you must have made a decision that you are going to become financially independent; you must have set the goal as to how much empire of wealth you want to build and when you hope to complete the building; and you must have made detailed plans as to what you hope to do or give in order to get the money coming. Thus it is taken for granted that you have already set the stage and the money has already started coming in. What then do you do?

As the money begins to come either in trickles or in torrents, there is the tendency for you to spend all your income, legitimately or illegitimately. This is normal in the light of Parkinson's Law, which states that "Expenses rise to meet income". But Brian Tracy believes that "you succeed financially to the degree to which you break Parkinson's Law." That is to say, "you do not allow your expenses to rise to meet your income, especially as your income increases." This means, to be able to accumulate money and become financially independent, you must form the habit of spending well below your income. Tracy suggests that spending 10 to 20 per cent less than you earn every single pay cheque will absolutely guarantee that you retire wealthy.

This issue of practising saving is one that needs not be handled with hands of levity. It is a habit that demands strong discipline and will-power, especially considering the varieties and myriads of wants that are competing for our very limited financial resources. But, just as Glenn Bland observes, to have much money, a person must be ready to do away with or forgo the acquisition of things. And the seemingly easiest way to resist the temptation of buying things is to develop and commit to a systematic saving scheme. This will tend to reduce your cash flow and, hence, help to check your expenses.

To illustrate the possibility of becoming a millionaire, Brian Tracy writes:

> If you were to save $100 per month from the time you started work at the age of 20 until the time you retired at age 65 and you invested that money in a mutual fund that yielded you an average of 10 per cent, you would be worth approximately $1, 118, 000 by the time you retire.

Thus Brian Tracy believes that "at $100 per month, anyone in America can become a millionaire".

Let us come home to Nigeria. If a man starts work or business at the age of, say, 30; and he disciplines himself to save just N100 every day; at 65, when he will retire, he would have saved N1, 277,500. And this figure is minus the interest that his money will earn him. Now, in the present Nigerian economy, N100 is not such a huge amount of money that a person cannot set aside, especially if the person has a source of daily or regular income. But the problem is that very many of us lack self-discipline and will-power in our society. And this is the reason why very many of us are still languishing in acute poverty.

In the opinion of Brian Tracy, "the first half of becoming wealthy is to earn the money, but the second half, the important half, is to hold unto it once you have earned it." And this is where the need for wise investment comes in. Tracy advises that we should spend at least as much time thinking about how to deploy our hard-earned money as we spend earning it in the first place. This is more so considering the high rate of ignorance displayed in the field of investment. So many people know a lot of tactics and techniques in the art of making money. But when it comes to the issue of seizing investment opportunities, they are next to illiterates. This calls for the need for everyone who desires to become wealthy to understand the intricacies of investments. Better still, everyone should employ the services of investment experts and consultants so that they will help him find ways of wisely investing his hard-earned money.

Granted that you have acquired some good knowledge of investments; or your experts or consultants have shown you some viable investment opportunities that you can go into. Good. But hold it! Take your time to study, research or investigate the viability of such opportunities. A Japanese proverb says, "Making money is like digging in the sand with a pin. Losing money is like pouring water on the sand." An idea that sounds too good to be true is probably not a very safe idea. Don't be on the lookout for easy money. To make real money, you must naturally, first of all, make cups or even buckets of sweat. Every good investment opportunity requires you to render some forms of services in order to earn rewards. If any investment opportunity does not require you to render services or give out something in order to earn profit, shun that opportunity. It is probably a sham. Besides, you must be careful about dupes and fraudsters. They abound in our present-day society. And they are seeking for every opportunity to swindle you and get hold of your hard-earned money. Be careful how you go about seeking investment opportunities. Endeavour to carry out feasibility studies of your investment opportunities. Above all, wisdom is the principal thing, and it is profitable to direct.

One other thing; resolve never to touch the money you are putting away, no matter what happens. This, in fact, is the most difficult aspect of the wealth building process. And it is the reason why many people still remain poor despite all their efforts and attempts to become rich. Of course, they have made a decision to become rich and wealthy; they have made plans as to how they hope to achieve this; they have even developed a strategy for a systematic saving scheme; and they have started saving money for the purpose of building an empire of wealth. But wait! Something happens, and they need cash badly. And what do you think they will do? Of course, they will remember that they have some money somewhere in the Bank. And off they go, with their cheque books or withdrawal vouchers. They will then withdraw some of that money which was meant for the purpose of wealth building. After they have spent that one, and the problem persists, or another problem arises, they will go back to withdraw, again and again, until the whole money gets finished. It is then they will realize what they have done, and they will resolve to start saving again, only to tamper with it later. And, before they know it, a full year has gone, and they have ended up saving nothing. Eventually, they begin to regret or wonder what they have spent the whole year doing.

It is in order for you not to have this kind of regret, year in and year out, and especially at the age of your retirement, that Brian Tracy counsels, "once you have begun a financial accumulation savings account or investments account, resolve that this money will never be used for anything except to create your own personal 'financial fortress'." In the opinion of Tracy, "This money represents your long-term future, and you should never, ever touch it." To touch it means having no meaningful future. This advice, in itself, is a very good one. But to be able to follow it through, you need to have a very strong self-discipline or an iron will-power. This is the only thing that will make you not to yield to the temptation of touching the money that you have in the Bank, especially when a very serious need arises. And if you are, like me, the type of person who can easily yields to temptation, then I advise that you develop some strategies that will help you to stay away from your savings. Remember, if you spend your savings now, you will have nothing to fall back to in the future. Therefore, save now and have a wonderful future; or spend your savings now and have a miserable future. The choice is yours.

By now you ought to have understood that wealth accumulation is a gradual and steady process. As Brian Tracy puts it, "it requires tremendous persistency and consistency. It requires that you work, save and invest, month by month, and year by year, for a decade or even two or three decades." In most cases, wealth building is a very painful exercise, one that requires great endurance and patience. But on the long-run, the rewards you stand to gain are nothing in proportion to the effort you put in. Just think about it. How will it look like when at the age of, say, 65 or 70, you retire from active service with your investments worth millions of Naira just because you are able to endure some hardship now and save for the future? How will you feel if, at the end of your life, you leave this world with the joy that you have not only provided for your family, but that you have something worthwhile to leave behind for their welfare after you are gone. But, on the other hand, how will it look like when, at your old age, you have no Kobo anywhere to fall back to, and you have to suffer untold hardship before you bow to the grave? Or, how will you feel if you have to leave this world with the knowledge that you have failed woefully in your responsibility of providing for your family, and that you have nothing to leave behind for their welfare? It will then be a very regrettable death for you. But it needs not be so. You can avoid this kind of scenario by making a strong decision to begin or join a systematic saving scheme towards building a solid empire of wealth for your own future and the future of your family.

# 20

## Use Other People's Money

In Mark Fisher's fable, the "Instant Millionaire" told the young man who was seeking for the secret of wealth: "Since time began, the rich have been using other people's money to amass their fortunes", and "Anyone really serious has never needed money to make money. By that I mean personal cash". This truth remains the same today. People are still using other people's money to run their businesses and are getting rich and wealthy therefrom. And if really you are serious about your resolve to build an empire of wealth, you cannot just rely on your meager savings; rather, you have to seek out a way of getting access to other people's money.

Some of the routes which you can go through to get access to other people's money include:

1. Commercial Banks: You can get short term working capital from commercial banks. What is required here is some valuable assets that can serve as collaterals for you. If you have these, do not be afraid to approach banks for loan. They will be willing to help once you are able to convince them that your ideas are viable, and your collaterals are valuable enough to liquidate the loan, in case of default.

2. Merchant Banks: Medium term loans for financing importation or procurement of raw materials, spare

parts and equipment could be got from merchant banks. Have the courage to knock on their doors if you need loan for any of these purposes. If you persist and do not get discouraged, I assure you that fortune will smile at you, as doors will begin to open for you.

3. Industrial Banks: Long term loans to finance machinery and industrial buildings and partly for the purchase of plant could be got from such industrial banks as Nigerian Industrial Development Bank (NIDB). Your dream can never be too big. If you fall into the category of great dreamers who have the idea and dream of running their own plants, then walk tall and knock on the doors of these industrial banks. You will be so surprised how easily the doors will open for you to collect your millions. Remember, these industrial banks are in business mainly to do this favour to would-be business moguls.

4. Individual or Corporate Financiers: There are some individuals or corporate bodies who are available to grant credit to business owners. If you need the help of such individuals or corporate financiers, just walk up to them and demand for the terms of their loans. If they are favourable, then avail yourself of that opportunity.

5. Founders' Share Capital: If your business is a fairly large one and your company is a limited liability company, and is quoted in the Stock Exchange, you can offer some shares to the public for subscription. The main thing is that you have the business idea, but that you incorporate individual or corporate financiers who will help with the funding and running capital. You don't necessarily need to own a

company hundred per cent before you can succeed at it. The idea is, give and it shall be given to you. That is, you give out part of your company in the form of shares and you get your needed capital for your business. The whole thing boils down to the age-long and time-tested principle of success: You can get what you want by helping enough other people get what they want.

6. Co-operative and Credit Societies: With your membership in a cooperative society, you can be given loan with which you can execute your business plans. Remember, a tree, they say, cannot form a forest. And it is through combined forces that a mad man can be overpowered. You cannot bear your burdens alone. You need other people's help. To speed up your progress, join a co-operative society and avail yourself of the opportunities therein.

7. Government Development Programmes: Government, through the ages, have always been very willing to give aid and support to Small and Medium Scale Enterprises (SMEs).Through such programmes as Operation Feed the Nation (OFN), Green Revolution, Directorate of Food, Roads and Rural Infrastructure (DIFFRI), National Directorate of Employment (NDE), The People's Bank, Better Life for Rural Women, Family Support Programme (FSP), and the attendant Family Economic Advancement Programme (FEAP), and the Women Support Initiative and the current Poverty Alleviation Program the Federal Government of Nigeria has made series of attempts to support current and would-be small and medium scale enterprises. And billions, if not trillions, of naira have, over the years, been disbursed for this

purpose. If you are a Nigerian and you have good business ideas and plans, it would amount to cheating yourself if you do not find ways to benefit from these well-meaning government empowerment programmes. And similar empowerment programmes exist in all other nations of the world. Try to take advantage of these programmes.

8. International Organisations: International organisations are not left out in their bid to help in the development of the Less Developed or Developing Countries. Such international organisations as International Labour Organisation (ILO), World Health Organisation (WHO), United Nations Economic and Security Council (UNESCO), United Nations Industrial Development Organisation (UNIDO), just to mention a few, have, over the years, come out with various programmes whose major targets are the Small and Medium Scale Enterprises (SMEs) in these countries. Presently, the services that UNIDO provides for SMEs include: training and consultation, technology acquisition and development, special trust fund scheme, industrial studies, information sources and networks, industrial investment promotion, etc. A present or would-be entrepreneur who is worth his salt would not hesitate in seeking for ways of benefitting from these mouth-watering international development programmes instead of relying solely on his meager, crude and time-consuming saving scheme.

9. Contributions or Loans from Relations, Friends and Brethren: This is probably the most common way through which people raise capital for their businesses. And it is for this reason that one needs

to be friendly and loving to all of one's acquaintances. One can never tell who will be used by God to pull one out of the ruts in the future. This confirms the following aphorism: "Remember to be good to the people you meet on your way up, you may need their help on your way down." Mind you, no condition is permanent. Don't despise people, or regard some people as unimportant, not matter how lowly placed. That poor cup-bearer of today may be the one to tell of your good points and recommend you to the king tomorrow. Be careful how you handle people. And if you have very good business ideas and plans, for heaven's sake, run to your relations, friends and brethren for help. They are about the only people who will confidently give you money with no strings attached.

Building an empire of wealth is a project that cannot be carried out with only your meager savings. You surely need other people's money to be able to complete such an enormous project. You must therefore take this issue very seriously and find ways of getting access to other people's money. This is one of the age-long secrets of wealth building.

# 21

## Be Faithful in Tithes and Offerings

Tithing is a practice that is ordained by God as a means of opening the windows of God's blessings for His children. In Malachi 3:10, God commands:

> Bring ye all the tithes into the storehouse, that there may be meat in mine house, and prove me now herewith, saith the Lord of hosts, if I will not open you the windows of heaven, and pour you a blessing, that there shall not be room enough to receive it.

Thus, to fail to pay your tithe is not only to rob God of His part in your income, but to also rob yourself of the blessings that come with the paying of tithe.

Every of God's children is in partnership with God. The covenant relationship that God establishes with His people also implies a partnership relationship. And just as God works with His children in spiritual matters, so also He works with them in their material and financial undertakings. And it is through the institution of tithe that God condescends to identify with the material pursuits of His children. It is through the paying of tithe that a child of God also recognizes and identifies with his partnership relationship with the Almighty God. Therefore for him to refuse to pay tithe is to refute, reject and renounce this divine/human partnership, as well as to cause the mighty hands of God to be removed from his business and financial undertakings.

In various parts of the Bible, God has promised to bless the works of our hands. An instance is Deuteronomy 28:1-14. Verses 11 and 12 specifically say,

> And the LORD shall make thee plenteous in goods, in the fruit of thy body, and in the fruit of thy cattle, and in the fruit of thy ground, in the land which the LORD sware unto thy fathers to give thee. The Lord shall open unto thee his good treasure, the heaven to give the rain unto thy land in his season, and to bless all the work of thine hand: and thou shalt lend unto many nations, and thou shalt not borrow.

Another instance is Psalm 1:1-3:

> BLESSED IS the man that walketh not in the counsel of the ungodly, nor standeth in the way of sinners, not sitteth in the seat of the scornful. But his delight is in the law of the LORD; and in his law doth he meditate day and night. And he shall be like a tree planted by the rivers of water, that bringeth forth his fruit in his season; his leaf also shall not wither; and whatsoever he doeth shall prosper.

Hence, ours is to work with our hands, and God's part is to bless the works of our hands. This is why we are told that except the Lord builds the house, they labour in vain that build it. Whatever we are doing for a living, if the lord is not with us to bless it, we may just as well be labouring in vain; we may just be like Peter, toiling all night and yet catching nothing. For, it is only when the Lord comes into the scene and takes control of the situation that we can catch a multitude of blessings. And what brings the mighty hand and the presence of God into our businesses, more than anything else, is our faithfulness in paying our tithe. It is not that God is interested in our money, but He simply wants us to acknowledge His role in the success of our businesses, as well as recognize Him as a part-owner of our businesses. In the business world, every partner in business, however small his contributions, is legally entitled to some part of the profit made. And since God sees Himself as a partner and, in fact, the key-player in our businesses, He therefore, through the institution of tithe, lays a legal claim to a percentage (10%) of the profit or income of our businesses.

One thing every child of God should know is that there are two personalities that are clamouring to go into partnership with him: God on the one hand, and satan on the other hand. That is to say, it is either you allow God to work with you, or you give room to the devil to operate with you. When a Christian identifies with God through the paying of tithe, he gives God the full responsibility of not only blessing the work of his hands, but also of helping to keep 'deboli', the devourer and the destroyer, from operating in his territory. On the other hand, when a person refuses to pay his tithe, he does not only receive the curse of God for robbing Him, but he also opens the door very wide for the devourer to come into his territory to destroy the fruits of his ground, and his labour. (Malachi 3:8-11). Every of God's children therefore has a choice to make, either to work with God, the Master-builder of our destiny, or to work with 'debolis', the devourer and destroyer of our God-given purpose. And it is the payment or non-payment of tithe that determines who he chooses.

Added to the issue of tithe is that of offering. Offering is what you give above the ten percent of your income. While the payment of tithe is compulsory, the giving of offering is not mandatory. Offering is what you give, as you will, in appreciation of the blessings of God upon your life. There is no stipulated amount or percentage of your income that you are to give as offering. You can decide not to give at all, and you can decide to give all that you have; you can decide to give little and you can decide to give much. The choice is yours

But what we need to stress here is that the rate of your giving is directly proportional to the rate of your receiving. This is what we found in Luke 6:38,

> Give, and it shall be given unto you; good measure, pressed down, and shaken together, and running over, shall men give unto your bosom. For with the same measure that ye mete withal it shall be measured to you again.

Therefore any Christian who wants to receive abundant of God's blessings through men cannot but give, give and keep giving. This is the number one secret of prosperity. And this is also the number one power that breaks the yoke of poverty.

Proverbs 11:24 describes for us two men who are distinguished by the rate of their giving:

> There is that scattereth, and yet increaseth; and there is that withholdeth more than is meet, but it tendeth to poverty.

To the natural man, it is prudence to keep what one has for oneself; but the man who is spiritually enlightened, and who has a mature mind, knows that it is more blessed to give than to receive. Hence he will not mind scattering all that he has among the less-privileged and the needy, as well as in the building of God's kingdom. But the end-result is that the person who keeps all that he has for himself will not have beyond that which he keeps; while the person who scatters all that he has around will be surprised to see the seeds he sowed germinate, grow and bear fruits; some thirty fold, some sixty and some a hundred fold. Poverty can never stand in the way of such a person who gives.

As you resolve to build an empire of wealth, the tendency is for you to become very thrifty, miserly and frugal. Yes, you will want to save virtually every Kobo that comes your way. But, much as we emphasize and encourage the practices of frugality, thrifty spending and systematic saving in order to succeed at building the coveted financial fortress, we, at the same time, discourage the habits of being miserly and stingy, as these will only place a limit on your chance of building an empire of wealth. You should therefore learn to give bountifully so that you can also receive bountifully.

# PART VI:

# RESOURCE MANAGEMENT PHASE

# 22

## Manage Your Time Wisely

Time management seems to be the most belaboured topic in the subject of self-development. Much has been said about it; volumes have been written about it; and innumerable ways have been advanced for proper time management. But in spite of all the efforts, time management is about the most ignored admonition that is given to man. This is particularly evident in the carefree attitude through which men fritter away precious time in unrewarding activities or inactivity.

If, as we have always been paradoxically made to believe, time is money, then we must exercise utmost care and prudence in spending it. After all, we cannot consciously and deliberately throw our hard-earned money into the bush. Ironically, much as we tend to equate the value of time with that of money, we continue to, consciously and unconsciously, waste it in reckless abandon. Yes, for the small minds, time is money, and it should be spent with prudence. But for the great minds, time is much more valuable than money, and it should be managed with utmost care.

Time is more valuable than money. Herein lays the great difference between the rich and the poor, the mediocre and the achievers, the obscure and the renown. This difference is inherent in individuals' attitude to time. Show me a man who has no regard for time, and who lazes about in wanton idleness, and I will show you a man who is sure to remain a pauper and a mediocre for life. On the other hand, show me a person who is so conscious of time that he orders his activities in order to meet deadlines, hit targets, and reach goals, and I will show you a person who is sure to achieve greatness in his chosen area of endeavours. Herein lays the difference between the man who will fulfil his divine purpose and calling and the man who will fail in his. Herein also lays the difference between the fulfilled man and the unfulfilled man; the accomplished and the unaccomplished; and between the happy and the unhappy man. Often, the difference is clear.

From the cradle to the grave, man's time is made up of time spans. It is made up of seconds, minutes, hours, days, weeks, months and years. Apart from the biblical account of how God stayed the time in Joshua's days, time has never been known to stand still. Right after creation, time has swiftly moved from seconds to minutes; from minutes to hours; from hours to days; from days to weeks; from weeks to months; from months to years; from years to decades; from decades to centuries; from centuries to millenniums; from millenniums to aeons; and from aeons to eternity. In the same way, immediately after birth, man's life has always moved swiftly from seconds to minutes, to hours, to days, to weeks, to months, to years, to decades, until he suddenly realizes that his time on earth is spent. In most cases, man belatedly realizes how time flies and often regrets his inability to do the innumerable things that he ought to have done. This and similar other write-ups on time management are coming your way so that you would avoid this kind of regret at the end of your life, especially if you are able to apply the principles that are prescribed.

For those who know, time management is one of the most important elements for succeeding in life. In the observation of Christian H. Godefroy and John Clark, authors of the *Complete Time Management System,*

> People who are noticed, who always end up succeeding brilliantly… are simply able to do a lot more things in a lot less time. And that's not all, not only do they do more things, they do better… And these super-gifted people take longer holidays too, and more frequently. Why? Because each one of them dominates the situation, because they know how to control their time, and exploit it to the full.

This observation contains unalloyed truth. This is more so bearing in mind the fact that everybody has the same twenty-four hours to work with. And while people in the above category make use of every second of their time, others fritter theirs away. And this brings about the differences in achievements between these two categories of people.

This leads us to the need to learn the secrets and techniques of proper time management. And the right question to ask at this point is, how should time be used? There are no hard and fast rules as to how time should be used. As pointed our earlier, so much has been written on the subject of time management; and so many strategies have been advanced for adequate time management. We cannot claim to be providing better and more workable strategies than those that have been given by the various experts. Rather, our intention here is to re-emphasize and remind ourselves of those techniques of time management that have proved most effective for many people over the ages.

**Take Time to Plan** – We are often told that, he who fails to plan invariably plans to fail. Planning is a management strategy that no individual or organisation can afford to neglect. Most often, time spent in planning is regained in ten to hundred folds through the great benefits that accrue from the exercise. If, as an individual or corporate body, you want to succeed tremendously, allocate quality time for planning. It is never a waste of time. It pays good dividends.

**Work through Plans** – It is one thing to allocate and spend time for planning, and indeed draw up the plans; but it is another thing to work through those plans. Some people can spend quality time making plans, but they never make use of them. This, unfortunately, is a big waste of time. If you have seen the need to make plans, then try as much as possible to implement them. And, for God's sake, stick to your plans! Exactly as you plan your work, work your plans. Do not deviate, unless it is extremely necessary. Your ability to stick to your plans will give you a sense of discipline, and a sense of self-confidence. Besides, you will achieve much more, especially as you will be less subject to distractions.

**Draw Up Activities/Time Schedules** – Activities and time schedules enable you to adequately account for how you spend every moment of your day. Your activities and time schedule could be on hourly basis – indicating what you spend every hour of the day doing. If you are able to draw up and stick to your schedule of activities, you will discover within a short time that you will become a master of your time, and there will be many rewards to show for it.

**Have a 'To Do List' Handy** – A 'To Do List' is a list of the important things that need to be done within the day. One expert suggests that you limit your most important tasks to only six per day. This, in his opinion, will enable you to concentrate on few very important things daily, rather than having to saddle yourself with a list of endless tasks that you cannot do. A 'To Do List' will help you to set your priorities right. With it, you will not need to waste your time on things that are not very important.

**Set Goals and Deadlines for Yourself** – When you set goals, targets and deadlines for yourself, you do not only have termination points for your tasks, but you also have a sense of purpose and of direction. Setting periodic (e.g. daily, weekly or monthly) goals or targets for yourself will enable you to work more effectively than just working without goals or targets. This will also help you to keep track of your achievements and successes. In the same way, setting deadlines for your various tasks will greatly exterminate the lackadaisical attitude often shown towards certain tasks or assignments. This is in the sense that when a person is confronted with the reality that the time for a particular task or assignment is running out on him, the person will have no option than to find ways of completing the task or assignment within the stipulated time. As a matter of principle, do not give yourself endless time within which to do things. Consciously set goals, targets and deadlines for yourself. This will enable you to accomplish much with your time.

**Have Enough Leisure Time** – All work and no play makes Jack a dull boy, so says the voice of wisdom. That is, after much labour, a person needs to take time off to rest. The time for leisure is not a wasted time. A person rests his nerves and recoups his lost energy within the time. It is also a time for recreation. To work continuously without giving yourself enough leisure is to work at a continuously diminishing rate. This is because even machines do get tired; that is why they often break down. Therefore if you work continuously without observing enough leisure, there is no gainsaying the fact that you are endangering your health and, like the machine, you will soon break down. Be careful. Work hard. But have enough leisure time. With it, you will always be bubbling with enough energy for your work.

**Employ the Time Others Waste** – Time and tide, they say, wait for no one. There is only one way to get ahead of others in this world; it is by making use of the time that others waste. Let us put it this way:

A successful person is the person

who prays while others are playing;

who works while others are waiting;

who studies while others are snoring;

who dreams while others are drinking;

who thinks while others are talking.

This is the portrait of a successful person.

Those minutes or hours you spend while travelling, riding a lift, waiting for an appointment, etc, should be employed for productive purposes. Others may waste them, but you can make good use of them. This is one of the things that will help you to get ahead of others in life.

**Avoid Unnecessary Visitations** – It is good to visit people; and it is good for people to visit you. But there should be time for everything; and visitation should be purposeful. A person who wants to make significant impact in life will not indulge in or encourage unnecessary visitations. It is better to plan your visitations in your activities/time schedule. And it is necessary that you let your visitors – relatives, friends, colleagues, neighbours, etc

– to know the period you are available for them to visit you. This is not being mean; rather, it is being time-conscious.

**Avoid Useless Discussions, Conversations and Arguments** – Some people can spend hours discussing or arguing about what is of no benefit to them. They talk about this and about that; and argue about so and so, until they realize that hours have passed without their knowing it. And the sad aspect of it is that they often end the discussions or arguments without something concrete to hold on to, or without reaching any compromise. Often, it is always a wasted time. A person who knows where he is going and what he wants out of life would have no time for insignificant discussions or useless arguments or conversations. Instead, he would invest his precious time for productive ventures.

**Concentrate on the Task at Hand** – This is where self-discipline comes in. Both the past and the future are of great importance to you. But it is better to concentrate on the present. Occasionally, you need to reflect on past experiences or to project into the immediate future. But this should not be at the detriment of the present task that you have at hand. All your energy should be channelled towards accomplishing the task at hand. This is what will help to ensure that you escape from the misfortunes of the past, as well as assure you of a better tomorrow.

Having come this far, we need to remind ourselves that you and I have only one life each, and a short time to live here on earth. Here, we do not have a continuing city; but our earthly tabernacles will soon be destroyed. It is therefore necessary that we do what we ought to do while it is called today; for tomorrow, we do not know what will become of our lives. And when we remember too that we will be remembered only by what we have done, then it is necessary that we do not only learn to redeem our time, but also to try to invest it for doing only those things that will last; so that when eventually we have passed on, and are forgotten, we will still be remembered only by what we have done!

# 23

## Employ the Help of Others

Two infallible truths: one, a tree does not make a forest; two, no man is an island. Have you ever come across a forest of one tree? For a forest to be called a forest, several trees must come together to form it. This is what makes a forest what it is – a congregation of trees. Let us recall, an island is a piece of land that is surrounded by water. In general sense, an island is anything isolated, detached or surrounded by something of a different nature. Hence, for a man to form an island is for him to isolate or detach himself from his fellow men; it is for him to be or stand alone.

As has been pointed out by good reasoning, it is not good for man to be alone. This is the reason why God in his divine wisdom decided to make a partner for him to be his help mate. Our subject here is not the importance of a life partner. Rather, we are confronted with the reality of the fact that to succeed every man needs the help of others. Life is such an intricate phenomenon that to succeed in life, each individual must of necessity employ the help of the other people around him.

A local adage says, "It takes combined force to over-power a mad man". In a way, life is likened to a mad man. To over-power and succeed at life, you need to combine your force or strength with those of others. To face life all alone is like attempting to over-power a mad man all alone. And that, as you know, is very risky.

Whatever you are doing, and whatever you are working at, you will achieve a greater amount of success if you employ the help of others. And one of the ways through which great men of old have done it is by building a network of experts around them. The veteran automobile emperor, Henry Ford, for example, did not possess high academic qualifications, yet he made a significant and lasting mark in the automobile industry simply because he was able to surround himself with a network of knowledgeable men from various disciplines. Even if you are highly educated, you cannot claim to be knowledgeable in all fields of learning and endeavours. This is the reason why you need to, like Ford, surround yourself with other men who are knowledgeable in those areas where you are deficient in knowledge. This is what networking is all about.

To be effective at networking, you must, first of all, be interested in people. A man who is always wearing a long, sullen face when he is with people will have great difficulty in networking with people. Yes, interest in people is a key factor in networking. To be a successful networker, you must consciously go out of your way to meet people, and you must habitually be delighted at seeing, meeting with or getting to know people. This is where the magic wand of successful people comes in. What is this magic wand? It is no other thing than wearing a beautiful smile when greeting and shaking hands with people. For God's sake, let your beautiful smile, your radiating and penetrating eyes and your firm and lively handshake show the fact that you are really delighted at meeting people. This is the never-failing secret of successful networking.

Life is so beautiful; and it will be much more beautiful if you do not make yourself a lone ranger. You do not have to struggle with life all alone. You need the help of your fellow men. And the most beautiful thing about people is that they are always willing to help. If you want to prove me, just go down the street right now, enter any house and ask any person you see for a cup of water. You will be surprised at the willingness with which the person will serve you the cup of water. That is just the nature of man; he is ever willing to lend a helping hand. You don't have to die of thirst amidst a vast oasis of living springs. Avail yourself of the help that is readily available to you.

As we talk about the need to employ the help of others, you should know the truth that others need your help as much as you need their help. This is because nobody is self-sufficient. You should also know that people are much more eager to help when they know that they stand to gain, in one way or the other, from what they are helping you to do. This is where the rather pragmatic slogan, "Nothing goes for nothing", comes in.

You should never be deceived to think that people want to help you because they like you. Rather, you should know that people are eager to help you because they know that one good turn deserves another. People will help you to do something when they know that there is something in it for them. Thus when you are trying to employ the help of another person in order to accomplish a particular task, the question that readily comes to his mind is, "What is in it for me?" If the person discovers that there is nothing in it for him, he withdraws his help. But if the person realizes that he stands to gain something from it, he throws himself unreservedly into the task for you. This is the secret of employing the help and assistance of others. And as a person who needs help or assistance from others, what you need to do is to recognize and make use of this WIIIFM or W3IFM bait. Learn to be unselfish, and let the other person see what he stands to gain if he helps to work at the task at hand or if he renders his assistance.

The culmination of it is the age-long secret of success: "Help enough other people to get what they want and they will help you to get what you want." The truth about success can never go beyond this. Stretch it any way or anyhow; it will eventually culminate at this infallible truth. As you are trying to build an empire of wealth, the questions that must keep ringing at the back of your mind are: (1) Who are those people who can help me to accomplish this goal? (2) What do they want, and how can I help them to get what they want? Your ability to supply the right answers to these questions is the first phase of your victory in your march towards building an empire of wealth. And the second and final phase of your victory comes when you consciously go all out to help enough of those people get what they want. It is only then that you will begin to get whatever you want out of life. This is because those people you are helping will have no option than to also help you to accomplish your heart's desire.

# 24

## Ask the Lord to Help You

We are told in Scriptures that except the Lord builds the house, they labour in vain that build it. This is plainly because except the LORD who is the Master Builder is allowed to play His part in building the house, it cannot stand. We should therefore not reject the LORD's willingness and offer to help build our coveted empire of wealth.

In the gospel according to St. John, Chapter 15 verses 4 and 5, Jesus, without mincing words, declared:

> Abide in me, and I in you. As the branch cannot bear fruit of itself, except it abide in the vine; no more can ye, except ye abide in me. I am the vine, ye are the branches: He that abideth in me, and I in him, the same bringeth forth much fruit: for without me ye can do nothing.

Yes, without God, we can do nothing. This is because it is in Him that we live, and move, and have our being. To live outside God is to be non-existent. And there is no way we can help ourselves without the help of the Almighty God. Many of us, like Peter, have toiled all night long at the 'lake' of business. Each time we draw up our net, it is always empty. In utter exhaustion, frustration and depression, some of us have given up 'fishing', and have washed and even hung up our 'net'. But if only we can invite the LORD to help us out of our fruitless toils!

Jesus is the Master of storms and the Master of the sea. He alone has the power and ability to walk on the sea without the water not giving way from underneath Him. He alone has the power and authority to command the wind and tell the sea waves to be still and they obey. Jesus alone knows the length, breadth and the depth of the treacherous sea. He knows just when and where to let down your net for a draught. He came to Peter's boat just at the time Peter had already given up hope and was washing his net in preparation to quit. In the same way, you may have given up on your situation, washed and hung up your net; you have even bidden good riddance to the drudgery of struggling to make a living; and the thought of building an empire of wealth. In short, you have quitted for good. But wait a minute! I have good news for you!

Right now, Jesus is standing by the sea side where you have hung up your net. And He is telling you, "Bring down your nets, and launch out into the deep, and let down your net for a draught." Forget about the fact that you have toiled all night and have caught nothing; forget about the fact that you have tried so many times and have failed. Jesus, the Creator of all creatures, knows exactly where the fishes are, and He is the one to tell you where to cast your net. All that is required of you is to obey His command. Rather than argue with Him, Peter, the failed and frustrated professional fisherman, simply obeyed Jesus's command, and he enclosed a great multitude of fishes. You also, if only you can let down your net according to Jesus's words, you will be surprised how much greater multitude of fishes you will catch.

Yes, when God, "which hath pleasure in the prosperity of his servant" (Psalm 35:27), comes into your boat and becomes a partner in your business, He gives you power to toil, and wisdom and direction needed for a successful draught. In anything you want to do, ask the LORD to help you. He is the Omniscient God who has the knowledge of how to do anything and everything. He alone is the person to help you.

Do you want to build an empire of wealth? Ask the LORD to help you build it. He is not only the Chief Cornerstone, He is also the Master Builder. He alone knows the plan, the right foundation to lay and the right block for the right position. Ask the LORD to help you, and you will come out with a strong and great empire of wealth that will stand the test of time. Shalom!

# BOOKS BY THE SAME AUTHOR

## Money Management/Wealth Building

- The Quickest and Smartest Way to Make Money
- Steps for Building an Empire of Wealth
- The One Dollar A Day Millionaire

## Inspiration/Motivation

- A to Z of Success Secrets
- Why Angels Fly
- The Power to Turn Your Life Around
- Understanding the Seasons of Life
- Peak Performance: A Pocketbook for Academic Excellence
- How to Improve Your Self-Esteem and Communication Skills
- Pathway to Personal Progress

## Academic

- English Language and Language Skills
- Language in Business Communication
- A Simple Approach to the Language of Literature
- Literature and Development: Perspectives from Stylistics

# ABOUT THE BOOK

## STEPS FOR BUILDING AN EMPIRE OF WEALTH

- Within the bindings of this book are the timeless and infallible principles that have aided all the great and wealthy men in ages past and present to build their vast empires of wealth.
- These principles have been proved and tested over the ages.
- These principles are guaranteed to aid you to successfully build your own empire of wealth.
- These principles worked for others.
- These principles will, no doubt, work for you too.

## ABOUT THE AUTHOR

LUCKY VINCENT is an academic and motivational writer, teacher, speaker, publisher and self-development expert who is charged with the task of helping to groom super successful people for the development of the human society in the 21st century and beyond.

The best graduating student of the Faculty of Arts and Social Sciences, Ambrose Alli University, Ekpoma (1995), Lucky Vincent (a.k.a. Vincent P.A. Obobolo) holds B.A. (Hons) English, M.A. English and PhD Linguistics (Stylistics). He is currently a lecturer in the Department of English Studies, University of Port Harcourt, Rivers State, Nigeria. With many academic and inspirational publications to his credit, and many more in the pipeline, Lucky Vincent is poised to storm the new millennium with a bang!